KNIGHTS OF BRAVELOVE

The Courageous Quest for Her Eternal Heart

Ed Hendricks

ISBN 978-0-692-15685-8
Printed in the USA

IN LARGER PRINT FOR EASIER READING AND BETTER UNDERSTANDING

ABOUT THIS POEM:

This is a "play post" (a PLAY, POem, and a STory combined) about time and how love spans the eternity of time. Add to these two, the greatness of God, the boundless heart of a woman and the courage of a man to love her wholeheartedly.

When I was young, King Arthur and the Knights of the Round Table always fascinated me. Their tales of bravery and heroic deeds made me hope that one day I could write a story about such things. I remember reading about them and my imagination would place me right there with them, taking on whatever may come with the same courage and valor they had.

Fast forward to my life today and it is through the gift of imagination and the power of love that I am able to write such a story close to being Arthur-like, but on a grander and more universal scale.

A second source of inspiration for this story came from the music of Jonn Serrie. In my first book ("Love, Sex, and Romance: Beautiful Love Poems for the Heart") I told of how Mr. Serrie came out with two CDs titled "Ixlandia" and "Midsummer Century." On both of those CDs, he introduced the concept of time and love. I was so inspired by the music behind this concept that I actually wrote a series of five poems and included them in my first book. (Those poem titles are "The Unfolding of the Two," "The Mystery of Destiny," "The Other," "From the Other Side of Time," and lastly, "The Eternal Expanse.")

I wrote Mr. Serrie and asked him if I could use his music as the source of my inspiration in the five poems and in this story. He agreed to my use of his music to inspire the poems I wrote. But also, his CDs have a character he created for them called The

Century Princess. She represents time and love itself and it is this character that gave me the idea for the queen of this play post. (Thank you SO VERY MUCH, Jonn Serrie! Your music stirs the soul and spirit.)

But imagination was not finished with me just yet. The idea of mixing an "Arthurish" tale with the concept of time and love came to me and I knew I had to write about it. I then "invented" some "suitors" for the queen. Though fictional, the characters in this ageless tale stands for those emotions it takes to love truly and deeply. I also wanted to use the gift that God gave me of writing poetry. So I wrote this play post using different poetic styles. Some may be not like what you are used to and have read before, but as with ALL my poems, you will easily be able to follow and understand what I am saying. I want everyone, not just a select few, to understand my words and their meanings.

This story also very spiritual in scope for I do believe it was God who created and put into each of us the capacity to not only love, but to love so deep and true. So I invented the names of "King Eternal" (or "The Eternal King") and gave them to him. I wanted a narrator in this story so I came up with one of God's loyal servant angels and gave him the name of Bold Eye.

But just like King Arthur and the Round Table Knights (and The Bible), these stories have a bad person in them. And so does this play post too. It includes a villain who wants to steal the joy of love from our Century Princess and fill her heart with the negative qualities of love: Pride, hate, jealousy, anger, confusion, and more. It is up to her "knights" to do battle with this villain, and turn her heart back to love once again.

And lastly, I strongly suggest that you read this play post with your bible and with my first book. There are references in this story that may confuse you, but both books will help to make my meanings more clear.

I hope this little tale of mine will inspire your imagination to love deeper and to always remember that love conquers all.

Best Wishes to all!

SPECIAL NOTE:

This play post is religious. It goes deep into The Bible with events that happened between God, Christ, angels, mankind, the devil and his demons. Various religions have different beliefs and interpretations about The Bible. What your particular religion teaches and what your personal beliefs are may not go along with what is in this play post of mine.

An example of this is some believe that while Christ was on Earth, he was God in the flesh and that he is God. Others believe that he was the first creation of God and that he is the son of God, thus making him a little lower than God. Two separate heavenly spirits. I chose to write this play post from the second point of view, that they are two different beings and God the father is greater than Christ the son. There are scriptures that point to both ways of thinking.

I appeal to you to just read with an open mind and heart. In The Bible, good wins over evil in the end and love always conquers hate. Those are the main themes of this saga, too.

Also, scriptural references are placed where they occur in this play post. I did this to honor God up front. References to my book and any others are placed at the end of my unusual play post of love and hope for the future.

DEDICATIONS

To Elohim God, and his loving son, our savior Christ. Words fall short in how I feel about their blessing me with the gift of poetry and the ability to imagine such a play post like this. I am forever grateful.

To the American Bible Society, the publishers of The New Revised Standard Version Bible (NRSV), and The Good News Bible (Today's English Version.) Both of these editions of The Bible helped me to create this play post. I am grateful that your organization bought the word of God to millions worldwide; myself included, and also made it easier to understand.

To my mother again, Ms. Dorothy B. Your encouragement was also the driving force behind the completion of this timeless play post. I thank you so much for your love and understanding.

To Mr.Jonn Serrie. Once again, I wish to express my sincere thanks for putting the concept of time and love into music. If you would have never done this, I would have never come up with the ideas for some of the poems from my first book, and to continue and expand on them in this second book.

To my local National Public Radio (NPR) station, KCUR 89.3. I thank you all for putting on the "Night Tides" radio program on Sunday Nights, hosted by Renee Blanche. It is the Night Tides show that I first heard the music of Jonn Serrie, and inspiration later took over. Also, I listened to both interviews you hosted by Young Adult Urban Fantasy author L. L. McKinney, and that her books "A Blade So Black" and "A Dream So Dark" are a retelling of the "Alice In Wonderland" story. I can relate to her in this respect because as I stated earlier, this book is a retelling of the King Arthur and the Knights of the Round Table legend.

To television host, author, and comedian Steve Harvey, who encourages all to "JUMP" from their present circumstances and do something new and different to change their life. I took your advice and took a BIG LEAP in the writing of this unique and exceptional play post.

To the actor/writer/director/producer/entrepreneur Tyler Perry. Your plays and movies have entertained millions, myself included. Your great faith and unlimited creativity has made you an extraordinary person. I tried to draw upon those very same powers of faith and creativity, to tell this extraordinary play post that honors both God and Christ.

To Marvel (©) and DC Comics (©). Both of your super hero characters such as The Avengers™ and Batman™ have inspired me since the 1970's. I have never forgotten the words "The Brave and the Bold" which DC Comics have described some of their characters as being. Decades later, I remembered those words as I was writing my play post and the naming of my characters Brave Duke, Brave Fire, Bold Eye and Bold Knight is the present-day result.

To George Lucas, (Lucasfilm (©) the creator of Star Wars (®) and all its later creations. The book about the movie "The Phantom Menace"* served as a guide to me in the writing of the war between Heaven and Hell. I am mainly a poet, and not a long form storyteller. So to imagine and construct a grand battle was difficult for me to keep straight and interesting. Also, the dual-bladed weapon that Queen Splendina fights with is based on the weapon the Star Wars character Darth Maul used to fight against the Jedi Knights.

To you, the readers of this play post. May it inspire you to love deeper than before, with an open mind and heart.

And lastly, this is an unusual dedication. There are some people in this world who choose to divide and use their thoughts, words, and actions to do so. They want their words of hate to cause conflicts, divisions and more. This is not the purpose of love, which unites hearts and minds for the good of all humanity. We are all equal in the eyes of God, and it's his eyes that are the most important of all.

If something in your soul is so dark that you wish to demean, bully, hurt, or even kill your fellow humans, then there is truly something inside you that needs changing. I urge you to let love in before it's too late.

Some may think that their words, actions, and power are tremendous. But the unlimited power of God and the infinite power of love are without a doubt . . .

STUPENDOUS!

* The book "Star Wars (®) Episode I: The Phantom Menace™" is published by Random House Publishing. Written by Terry Brooks. Based on a screenplay and story by George Lucas.

FOREWORD

In March of 2015, I started to write this incredible story. But months earlier, I was putting it together on paper and in mind. Because of the very unusual nature of this story, (play post) and the rules I broke in its writing, I felt any traditional publisher would not accept it. So just like my first book, I self-published this one too.

In March of 2018, I finished the writing part and started to put the whole book together. Three years of disappointments, disruptions, setbacks, and even failure. The devil interfered in many ways, seeking to make sure this book would not be written AND to disrupt the construction of it as well. But God had mercy on me and kept "telling" me to keep going, and to have faith in him to the finish. Writing this book has taken me on a personal journey of the soul and spirit. It has made me stop and think about my own future eternal destiny very much.

I have made many mistakes in my life, and will make them until the day I die. But with age comes wisdom, and a sign of wisdom is learning from past mistakes. I believe it was God's blessing and grace that have forgiven me for the past, and gave me the gift of inspiration to write this story (play post)

It is my sincere hope that the word of God and the message of this book will help you, the reader, to know that love conquers all and very soon the love of God through his son will conquer all forever. If you have felt in your life that love has left your heart and turned you into a "Dark Soul," then maybe The Bible and a fantastic love story like this will help to change your heart, like it has done to me.

And lastly, in the writing of this play post, I unwittingly created some of the most powerful "super heroes" ever imagined. Why can I make this claim? Because Queen Splendina and The Knights of Brave Love powers comes from the very hands of both God and Christ. I don't think you can get any more higher or any more powerful than God and Christ.

A PAGE OF THOUGHTS.

"Do not be afraid what the devil will cause you to suffer. . . Be faithful, even until death, and I will give you the crown of life". Revelation 2:10 (Scripture shortened)

"Old myths, old tales of bravery, old heroes have never totally died out. They are simply sitting at the bottom of our minds, waiting to rise once again."

"There's love and then there's war
Sometimes you have to go to war for love"
(Richard the Deep Hearted says to Dark Soul)

"Like the tales of knights so old
Brave at heart, with courage so bold
My love for you is a story that must be told

But loving you is not a fairy tale
It's a feeling I know so well
And in my heart is where it dwells

You are my queen, I am your knight
Like a hero, for your love I will fight
Even when my mind turns off its light"*

We are never too old to learn something new, and never too young to learn something old.

*From my poem "The Queen of My Dreams," in my book "Love, Sex, and Romance: Beautiful Love Poems for the Heart."

TABLE OF CONTENTS:

May I now introduce the characters of my play post.

King Eternal (The Eternal King) – Is none other than God himself. The creator of ALL things in, above and below the heavens. And the inventor of love. It is because of his wisdom that we all are here and also why I am able to create such a story like this. It is my most sincere wish that I tell this in such a way that honors and gives him the glory he is always deserving of.

Jesus Christ - The "Faithful and True Son of God." The savior of humanity and a key figure in the telling of this tale. It is Christ also I strive to honor with my play post.

The Holy Spirit - Empowers the knights to do extraordinary feats. Under the direction of God and Christ, impossible things are accomplished.

Bold Eye The Archangel – Bold Eye is a name that I came up with which I feel is in tune with the title of this play post. He is God's loyal servant and our narrator. I felt I needed "someone" to keep things in order, to help this story flow better, and to make it easier to understand at times. Also, there are events that will happen in heaven that need to be explained as this story is being told. Bold Eye also has many loyal and faithful angelic brothers that will soon be called into battle, to uphold the sovereignty of heaven.

The Century Princess/Queen Splendina – She is the main character here and everything revolves around her. She represents all women . . . past, present and future. The deep, splendid love inside a woman's heart, and her yearning to share it. Also, she stands for time and love both, as the Jonn Serrie CD's explain. The eternity within. The Century Princess begins as passive in my tale, but as love itself and its creator is questioned, mocked, and then stupidly challenged, The Century Princess is changed into Queen Splendina, who is God's ferocious defender of women and eternal love.

Richard The Deep Hearted – Is the one who loves our princess through time and whose love for her has no limits. Boundless . . ageless . . . unfailing . . . eternal love.

Sir Romance A Lot – Is in love with our princess so very much. He adores, admires, cherishes, devotes, treasures, romances our noble lady.

Brave Duke – Is a protector of our princess's heart. Will do everything within his power to make sure her heart is happy and content. Also has a younger "brother" who is even more protective than he is.

Bold Knight – The main protector of The Century Princess's heart and emotions. Together with his older "brother" Brave Duke, they represent the boldness it takes to love wholeheartedly. Respect, bravery, confidence, integrity is some of the qualities he stands for. Very, very determined to protect his lady. He is the leader of the knights and quite outspoken.

Prince Passion – Is the lover of our princess. He represents the physical parts of love. Believes in making love to her mind first, then her body. He stands for affection, tenderness, caresses, romance, fantasy, and then the act of making love.

A Man – Is ALL the knights gathered together inside himself. Each knight is just one part of the whole mind of a man who wants and longs to love a woman as deeply as she wants to be loved, and as deeply as she wants to love him back.

Dark Soul – The evil character in my play post. He hates The Century Princess and all the finer emotions of the heart. Always seeks to strike her down and make her feel badly. Hate, pride, jealousy, fear, mistrust, anger, confusion, and many others like these are what he has in his arsenal. Will do battle with the knights to see if he can turn her heart from everlasting happiness to eternal sadness. But Dark Soul has a much more sinister purpose in mind. A purpose so selfish and evil that it could affect the eternal destiny of all humanity.

Dark Soul also has many hordes of his evil brothers that will help him in his attempt to defeat Queen Splendina and her knights.

PART 1. INTRODUCTIONS (And Disruptions)

THE ETERNAL KING, ELOHIM GOD SPEAKS FIRST.

My Children
All my beloved children
Lend to me your eyes and your hearts
Your souls and your spirits
Listen to the words of the one I have inspired
For through him I have a wonderful story to tell

I am the beginning and the end of all things
The end and the beginning of that which is to come

Grand creator, wonderful inventor of love I am
For it has flowed through me forever
I created my son and your savior Christ from it
I formed each of you from its vision
And my image

Gather your minds to the telling of this imaginative story
For my inspired one has my blessing to write it

Know that my mind is unsearchable
My thoughts limitless
My wisdom fathomless
And my love timeless

Know that I am the beginning and the end of this story
And of many more to come.

The Eternal King and his son, The Lord Christ.

Greetings humans of this realm
Before you all I come with a magnificent story
Of faith, hope, and the greatest of all, love

BOLD EYE THE ARCHANGEL I am called
For I act with boldness wherever my eyes gaze
Sent to do the bidding of my Lord and his faithful son

Named from the inspired imagination of this author
Created I was to guide you through this mythical tale

But I have been here for millenniums
Watching, observing
I have seen the best of love since mankind began, and time has
passed
And sad to say, I have also seen the worst of love

And I wonder . . .

Love that has created life
Love that has taken life

Love that has taken its owners to my dwelling place
Love that has put its owners into the ground

Love that was meant to be
Love that was not

Both sides of love I have watched play out through time
Both sides mankind has spoken and sang about
Written about

Come with me as I guide you through this fantastic fable of
fantasy and imagination

For today this writer wishes me into his world
And I gladly accept

My only wish is for you the reader and the thinker to open your minds up fully
And your hearts as well.

THE CENTURY PRINCESS introduces herself.

Eons ago before the keeping of time began
I was created by an extraordinary man

King Eternal, the king and creator of this universe
Also known as God, the last and the first

From the unsearchable depths of his thoughts
I was conceived and brought forth

I represent the deepness of time and love
Both names are immortal, like "The One" above

Blessed to be brought forth from imagination divine
And the deepness of love and eternity combined

Love fills my heart with so much happiness
That overflows into my soul and causes me much bliss

It glows within me like the stars and the sun
Making me feel their creator and I are as one

Through space, time, and eternity
The power of love has set me free

Free to give ageless love, and for it to receive

Free to feel its unlimited power and believe

Oh, what wonderful joy love brings to me
It shines through my eyes of forever (1) for all to see

Words sometimes fall short about how love makes me feel
Such a delightful emotion that is so very real

A heartfelt thanks to King Eternal, who created with care
The endless gift of love, which he unselfishly does share

Love's beauty, splendor, and all its glory
Is why I was created now, to tell this story

BOLDEYE THE ARCHANGEL: You have been introduced to
The Century Princess, whose heart spans space, time, and is
the vastness of love itself. Now let's meet her "knights" who
guard her heart and serve her faithfully.

My everlasting princess, my lady, my best friend
It is I, RICHARD THE DEEP HEARTED
And it is so very good to be with you again

I am in love with you so much and so deep
From sunrise to sunset and beyond the midnight
And even when we sleep (2)

Throughout all the ages and eons of time
I have always deeply loved you
To your heart I have always been kind

I have always answered your heart's deepest calling
Unfailing, without question
In love with you I am forever falling

Countless ages and millennium after millennium
Together with the stars
I feel my love has always been

Inside the mind of a deep loving man I exist
For that is the man that you deserve (3)
Such a true man your heart cannot resist

Before your heart I now appear
Loyally, faithfully
To take away all your love fear

So my love, never forget I am always here
NEVER will I leave
To your heart I want to make this very clear

Remember my lady; my first duty is to God, and his faithful son
The creator of life and love
But I will serve you all, until my life's course is run

For your heart's call I now await
With patience and undying love
I promise to you I will never be late

SIR ROMANCE A LOT introduces himself.

My noble empress,

An adorable princess, you be
And a beautiful lady, you are to me
Stunning and lovely for ALL the universes to see
For loving you fills my heart with glee

May I introduce myself to this plot

Ed Hendricks

It's I your humble and honourable Sir Romance A Lot
And I love you with ALL I got

My love for you comes from deep, deep within
Placed there inside by The One without sin
The Lord above who has always been

Royal lady, with skin so fair
With eyes of forever that have always been there (4)
An ever-loving heart, that is full of care

I too, feel I have loved you before the keeping of time
An endless longing in this heart of mine
Here today with you, time and love combine

Precious lady, my love is so intense
I feel my love for you in every nerve and sense
Totally one hundred percent, never on the fence

Like my brother knight who has spoken before
I too, have so much love in store
To you I am willing to give even more

Even until my last breath
I will faithfully love you, until there's nothing left
And then take this wonderful feeling into death (5)

When my spirit goes back to The Eternal King
It will also tell him about this thing
Of how much joy to you I did bring

So my beloved lady, never fear
To your heart I will always be near
And it's calling I will forever hear

BOLD KNIGHT introduces himself.

My lovely queen
It's I, your steadfast servant Bold Knight

Sworn by a sacred loyal oath to love you
With honor and respect
But mostly with courage

For it takes true courage to love you completely
With everything inside me
And then some

To always reach deep within and bring out
More honor, more respect
And again, more courage
For you are worth the effort

My lady,
It is your precious loving heart and the vast love that fills it
That I will give my life to protect
And at the same time unselfishly love
Always and forever

Those who try to break your gentle spirit
With negativity, jealousy
Stupidity, Idiocy
I will deal with in my own way
Again, your heart is my greatest concern

So much I am in love with you
As with my other "knights"
Though different, we all have the same purpose
This is to love you wholeheartedly

My feelings go beyond what is normal
An ordinary man cannot love you as much as I love you
For it is true, raw courage
Determined and relentless bravery
That guides my path on the journey of love
Its final destination is your heart

Our King has given me extraordinary valor to be in love with
An extraordinary lady and queen as yourself
All glory and honor goes to him

BOLD KNIGHT'S OLDER BROTHER, BRAVE DUKE, introduces himself.

As my young brother just said
He loves you deeply, with heart and head
And so do I

Brave Duke is my title
To me, your love is ever so vital
It is as necessary as breathing fresh air

I may have a title of nobility
Duke I am called, but brave I be
Because bravery is my nature, my character

Sworn I am also to protect your heart
Your soul, your spirit, your mind also takes part
All of me safeguards all of you

To your defense will always come Bold Knight and I
Never will we leave you and say goodbye
Eternally I am here for you, my sweet
You are the one that makes my life complete

Loving you with unwavering courage has made me so strong
Another reason why I have loved you so long
You have always been my queen of many a century
Shining, glowing for all to see

My eyes have gazed upon all your ways
In my mind, a picture of you constantly plays
Never ending thoughts of pure delight

So my love, my lady, my beautiful queen
I thank you for letting me love you with a heart so clean
From King Eternal with strength, boldness, and raw courage

PRINCE PASSION makes his presence in this saga known.

Ah, my sexy lady,

It is I, Prince Passion, your forever lover
It's your sensual secrets I long to discover

The one who loves, craves, and desires only you

I have loved you since woman first met man
Truly and deeply, with all that I can

Now my love for you has turned to desire
Only by us making passionate love will quench this fire

I find you so alluring and sensual
In certain parts of me, you always make the blood flow

In his book titled "Love, Sex, and Romance"
The Human Ed wrote the poem, "Instant Sex, Always Love"

Ed Hendricks

His sultry poem raises my excitement for a chance
The chance to . . .
Fondly stare into those eyes of seduction
Gaze upon your nakedness with hunger
Delicately kiss your lips of lusciousness
Taste your natural nectar so sweet
Make love with you as one

Making love with you until there is no strength left
Then to hold you close, as we catch our breath

Afterglow, afterglow, afterglow (6)
That feeling of total satisfaction that pleases us so

My Princess of the Centuries,

I am your timeless lover, as you can see
And it's your body I want to set free

I have loved and longed for you so fine
Feelings that have grown stronger in the passing of time

Now today, as love and lust shine
So happy I am that you are mine

To your heart, I too, will always serve and protect
To your body I want to always lay next

To your soul, I will always love blind
I want to make love to ALL of you, including your mind

Your eternal lover I will always be
Awaiting your call, whenever you need me

SPECIAL AUTHOR'S NOTE:

At this particular section, I wish to apologize for the sensuality I am using to describe Prince Passion's feelings for his dear Century Princess. And for future thoughts like this he will express.

You may be thinking now that why such language is included in a story that honors both God and Christ, and the emotion of love? And why are there "men" swearing an oath to love their princess?

I ask you the reader to again just read on with an open mind and heart. Please have faith that these questions and many others your mind may have formed since you first started reading my play post will be answered.

Ed Hendricks

The Century Princess

It's I again, THE DAUGHTER OF KING ETERNAL

With a heart full of gratitude I want to express

To tell my knights who love me so true
How much I appreciate all of you

You all have my love, admiration, and respect
A mirror to your souls, those feelings reflect

Because of your love, courage, and dedication I am impressed
I know for sure I have been wonderfully blessed

And to my "lover" whom for only me he lusts
You too have all my love and trust

My heart sings loudly with joy inside
Through space and time, it effortlessly glides

It goes to the very presence of the Eternal King
Along with the angels, it also now sings

How can I ever thank my knights
Whom for my love they zealously fight

How can I be -----

"What is all this nonsense about love?
When it is just a useless emotion
A waste of time and thought
And it does away with good and common sense
Something I feel you humans can do without.
Just leave it in the hands of whoever claimed to create it
And let him deal with it all by himself

I just don't see the sense it makes
For I too have witnessed love's little good
But mostly bad and evil

It seems to be more unpredictable and unreliable
Something for the weak of mind
And stupid at heart"

BOLD EYE asks: What's this foolishness? An accuser of love? How dare he interrupt our Royal Highness and tell our King Eternal to just keep his creation to himself. Who is this madman?

THE CENTURY PRINCESS ASKS:

Who are you with a heart so black
And why is it the beauty of love that you lack?

DARK SOUL is the name I am known by
And unlike the Archangel Bold Eye

I was NOT sent from that one above
To turn your heart into white doves

More like an uncaring crow is what I bring
To silence your heart, and make it not sing

I too, have been here for a long time
And I just do not think that love has been kind

I have seen little good, and mostly bad
And it does not make my heart sad

It should have never come from "that thing" on Heaven's throne

KNIGHTS OF BRAVELOVE

He should have left it inside himself alone
But since he stupidly did not, and now it's here
I see it causes jealousy, mistrust, and LOTS of fear

Also many other negative emotions
The lives it costs could fill the ocean

I side with those who think it is a waste
Of time, thought, and even faith

I am here to disrupt it inside every woman and man
To make them all see things my selfish way, is the plan

Century Princess . . . no . . . Cursed Cow, your new name shall
be
That is the name that makes more sense to me

Cursed Cow, you say it's time and love you stand for
In my mind, those things are such a bore

I focus on the worst of love and its aftermath
And believe me "Not a Lady," it's no shining path

Time and time again
I have seen love change to an enemy, which was first a friend

Love that started off with praises and songs
Ended up being so very wrong

Love that turns one into its slave
Love that puts its lover into the grave

Wasp face mistress, you have watched all of this too
You know the words I speak are true

And how love turns hearts to blue
Finally, Cursed Cow Princess who claims to love so true
Who are these "fools" in love with you?

THE CENTURY PRINCESS:

Woe, woe, woe
It is sadness that I now know

I admit that Dark Soul you are right
For I have witnessed what you say, in my sights

I too have seen much heartbreak
And how one life did another take

I have seen what started so glad
But due to fear and mistrust, turn to sad

I have looked upon the worst of jealousy
And just how bad it can be

How much have I witnessed true love turn to hate
What started as destiny, turned to fate

Dark Soul, why do you say these bad things?
Great sadness to my heart, your words now bring

BOLD EYE: "A "hater" in every sense of the word has made his presence known, and has saddened the princess very much. But what do our knights have to say about Dark Soul and his slanderous accusations? Read on and let's find out.

Also dear reader, I am now joined by my faithful angelic cherubim brothers, The Ark of the Covenant protectors Gold

Wing and True Flier, as well as Faith Speak, who have taken an interest in this tale of love for this age and beyond.

BOLD KNIGHT: Dark Soul, HOW DARE YOU mock The King of Eternity with your horrible words. You call him "That Thing?" And to call our gentle empress Cursed? Not A Lady? Cow? YOUR CRAZY words have made her heart melancholy by such scorn.

The wonderful damsel whose heart I steadfastly serve
And faithfully guard

What gives you the right to utter such nonsense?

Your very name reveals the color of your heart
Your mind and your soul too

As with a coin, there are two sides
While your choice is to tear down
My choice is to build up and protect
While you choose unhappiness
My companions and I choose delight and joy

From what rotten part of Hell do you come from with this ridicule?

RICHARD THE DEEP HEARTED:

My brother is full of truth
Dark Soul, your name means your heart and your soul are dark
And that is where I will start

Dark Soul, you have stupidly chosen
A heart the color of the darkest night

This tells me nothing inside you loves the light
We swear to love and protect our dearest one
To exalt love's beauty in her sight
Now you bring her jest and fright

I hear the idiocy of this knave
And I wonder . . .
Why is it hatred that you crave?

Your unkind words seek to destroy
While I choose to build up
And bring much joy

To watch over the heart of heart of my lady so true
The queen of my dreams (7)
Isn't that what we deep hearted men do?

While your words insult
My words honor and cherish
So happy am I for their result

As I said before, my love goes so deep
Like the eternal flowing tides of the ocean
Deeper than the dream-filled realms of sleep

Dark Soul, why is your soul so dark?
It resembles a thousand and one nights
Its true nature is now so stark

SIR ROMANCE A LOT:

From the far flung galaxies
To the center of life today
I am now totally in love with "The Other" (8)

"The Other," being my grand lady
Who loves so pure, so natural
And who I love back the same

I lift my hands to the heavens and sing psalms of praise
To the Eternal King for his infinite blessing of love
As those who love him have done and still do today

Life is work and love is rest
It is my life's work to love my divine Sultana
As time has passed, I've passed test after test

But you, oh cruel and mean, Dark Soul
Because your love has grown dark
Of your foolishness I want no part

What turned your heart from the sun at noon
To the time of day that reveals the moon?

I wonder about your past fate
What caused your change, from love to hate?

DARK SOUL:

"What's it to
ANY of you
What I do?

You all just need to know
I now hate love so
And it forever, must go

To love, I am no friend
Nothing good to it, I will lend

Ed Hendricks

All my energy and actions I will spend
To put it to a final end

I will use all my dark power
Every day, every hour
Until your Lemon Lady Love is made sour

By using sarcasm, ridicule, and spite
Taunting, scorn, and the like
Her heart will know fear and fright

I will put in her such a scare
That she will never, ever dare
To lay her heart open so bare

I have MANY sinister powers I will use
To make her soul sing the blues
And make love "yesterday's news"

Why, I can even use yesterday's *and* today's news
To give her heart and mind the blues! HA!

So much of my contempt comes from humanity
From what I hear and see
Throughout all of human history

I then gather up all of this
Leaving out any bliss
And shoot negative "arrows" at her that won't miss

Time will soon tell what I really have in store
For you foolish knights of this lore
And believe me, it won't be a bore
This crazy crocodile you faithfully adore

I will intimidate and frighten more and more
Until her heart is totally on the floor

BOLD EYE: Ah . . . this dark villain of the heart has revealed some of his sinister purpose. He wants to absolutely crush the heart of our lovely princess. What else does he have on his twisted mind? Also, my loyal brother Faith Speak has left to go tell some of our other angelic brothers what is happening here. Sometimes, he just talks too much.

THE CENTURY PRINCESS:

Dark Soul, why are you so mad
To change a heart that was so glad
And make it now so sad?

Through all the passing ages of time
Love's beauty and splendor were always mine
But you now have taken them away

Like a true thief in the night
You have stolen my love light
And replaced it with your own dark heart

Now my days are so gloomy
For what you have spoken is so vicious to me
My spirit is the color of yours

I feel as if heaven's door
Which was so open with its magnificent light before
Is now closed, along with its glory

Oh Dark Soul, how could you be so vile
And take away the feeling that makes me smile?

My tears now fall through space and time

BOLD KNIGHT:

Madman! Fool!
Dark Soul, you have the mouth of a roaring lion
But the true heart of a mouse
For only a heart and mind so small
Would utter such idiotic things
And think of love the way you do

So angry I am with you
Your words drip with bitter poison
From a mouth so wretched and a mind to match

A soul darker than the far reaches of space
And the color of dirt

Just because your heart is so dark
Does not mean you have to share its color and reveal its nature
to all
Keep that negativity to yourself and those like you

YOU are "that thing" that should be under the feet of King
Eternal
YOU are the crazy one and NOT our beloved empress
For she radiates love, beauty, and light
Which attracts true hearts
While you stupidly spread hate and fear

Why don't you be like the mouse you really are
And go away very quietly

BRAVE DUKE:

A madman you have been earlier titled
And a madman you will always be
For now and through eternity

Your thoughts about love
Are full of contempt and scorn
Not from King Eternal were they born

From your own twisted imagination
Inside your deceitful mind
You say what is not kind

What are the reasons for your rudeness?
Maybe you too have suffered heartbreak
And its pain you could not take

Maybe in the past, love for you was real
Then another came along, and her love he did steal

Maybe you did have a loving wife
But the passing years finally took her life

Whatever reasons that may be
For your unrelenting cruelty

You have not an ounce of right
To fill our queen's heart with so much fright

PRINCE PASSION:

I love my attractive lady, naked or clothed
Holding nothing back, I am very bold

Mind and heart, body and soul

I take her to a place, where she loses control

My love brings her back from ecstasy's highest peak
I caress and hold her, as we fall asleep

Yes, I am in love with the one I adore so much
And it's not only her body I desire to touch

Her mind, her soul, I long to caress with care
She will be content knowing I too, will always be there

Her eternal lover I am, yes that's true
But Dark Soul, don't underestimate me, I can and will fight too

Like my best friends, and brother knights
I stand tall for what is right

You, whose heart is the color of night
Puts inside me not an ounce of fright

Instead, you bring out of me more courage so brave
It's her love and dignity I fight to save

My greatest battles are for the honor of the Eternal King
Glory to him first, I always want to bring

My Lord the King Eternal and his son so faithful
Blessed me with their love and I am ever so grateful

But you, whose soul is so dark hearted
Have picked a fight that you should have never started

How dare you all these wild accusations bring
Against my lovely queen and The Eternal King

IT IS YOU that's the crazy one
You need to take your scorn, and run, run, run

Run back to the dark hole you crawled out of
And don't come out until your heart knows love

You are nothing more than a madman and a bully
That my brother knights and I will deal with fully

The love for our king and our queen stands firm
We will not crawl away from you, like a worm

Instead we will battle you with the strength of a lion
It's YOU who will turn and run, with eyes crying

So Dark Soul, what will you now do
You now know for sure WE WILL fight you

DARK SOUL:

Prince Passion, you utter lies and empty promises
Who are you to challenge me?
Who are ANY of you so-called knights to question me?

Irritated I am at your words, Prince Passion
But my feelings spread to all you delusional knights
Delusional because you dare to oppose me
If you want a fight, hell's fury is what I'll give
An arsenal of weapons I have, a battery of fearful emotions
They have served me very well throughout time, and rarely do they fail

Here is one weapon I named "The Dragon"
My dragon spits the other 3 D's: Despair, Distress, and Doubt

Its venom has poisoned many souls of humanity
Now that includes your dog-ear princess

Prince Passion, you claim to love that mule woman
I think you just want her body only
Your own self-indulgence you want to satisfy
Centuries upon centuries I have seen men use women
Caring nothing about their minds, craving only their bodies
Men have used them for their own needs and greed
Sometimes in unspeakable ways

I have seen sex used as weapons of war on and off the battlefield
And I laugh loudly

How do you humans explain rape? Degradation? Sexual torture? Strange lusts?
The practice of FGM? (Female Genital Mutilation) Prostitution?
Your creator NEVER invented these. YOU HUMANS DID!
I am so happy to see your depraved ways
It actually shines a bright light in my dark heart! HA, HA, HA!

You knights are so dim-witted
Thick-headed, thoughtless

You all say you honor your Eternal King first
Whom I detest with everything inside me
Then that hen queen you "claim" to love
Well, I "claim" and "know" you don't
You all have your own self-interests at heart

Richard the Deep Hearted and Sir Romance a Lot
You both claim to love her so deeply, so totally
But you really love her blindly and stupidly

I notice your stumbles in your ways
Your doubts, fears, insecurities are before my eyes too
True knights you are not
But users of your crow face bird's mind
For your own twisted benefit
Mankind has followed your pitiful example
And copied your misuse of emotion
You two knights have set these low standards
Once again, I laugh large
True love supposedly never falters
But you two fools have, and always will fall

To the "brothers" Bold Knight and Brave Duke
Who "claim" to be so brave
I have seen your doubts and fears too
Both of you have stumbled and fallen many a time
This time you really are mistaken in your opposition of me

Unlike the mythical knights of human legends
You two are gutless, mud dwelling creatures
Faint of heart, like your king
And your silly "lady"

Courage is not your friend, but fear and fright are
Even now as I speak, I sense your spirits quiver
I feel your hearts tremble
Still again, I smile in victory

All of you knights' real "claim" is to cowardice
And you are putting on a false front
Pretending to love your King Eternal and your crazy princess
So they will bestow their gifts upon you
For your own selfish interests
Traitors . . . cowards . . . counterfeits

You all seek your own glory and not of those two impostors in heaven you serve

BOLD EYE: What's this mess? Dark Soul has let loose his "dragon". A speech that burns with the fire of hate and venom of a madman. He has made reckless and insane accusations not only to our knights, but against the Eternal King and the lovely Century Princess. How dare he question the loyalty of our knights and then to mock the Eternal King himself? He has truly gone mad. How will our daring knights "slay" this dragon? They have battled and defeated many of the most terrifying physical dragons in the past, including one of the most hideous and dangerous beasts of all time, the monstrous Terrorwolx. (Pronounced as "Terror Walks")

How will they defend the sovereignty of Elohim God? Let's read on to find out what God has blessed his inspired poet, the writer of this saga, to reveal to us.

Also, my faithful brother Faith Speak has returned and with him are the legions of angels known as The Dreadnaught Warriors. Fiercely loyal and fearless, they have no fear whatsoever and have fought many a battle against their former brothers, and now apostates who left heaven forever. Their fearlessness is legendary in the realm above the stars.

They are led by the Seven Supreme Seraphim, who are seven of the many very powerful angels that are at the throne of God giving him praise and glory. But they also have other duties as well, and have gone to war for their King Eternal. It was two of the Seven Supreme Seraphim and the Dreadnaught Warriors that surrounded and protected the prophet Elisha. (2 Kings 6:8-18) It was also *all* of the Seven Supreme Seraphim's that poured out the symbolic seven bowls of God's anger in your bible book of Revelation. (Revelation 16)

MEANWHILE, IN THE GREAT CELESTIAL THRONE ROOM OF KING ETERNAL, THE SON OF MAN, THE GLORIOUS LORD JESUS CHRIST, SPEAKS FOR THE FIRST TIME IN THIS EPIC TALE.

Abba, (Father) we have been witness to and have heard both sides of this story so far. The courage of the knights has greatly impressed me. Their accuser hurls brash accusations at them, but they stand firm in their resolve to honor and serve you. Then to love their princess. They amaze me and make my heart glad. I think you feel the same too.

But I know their accuser **VERY** well and know his crafty tricks. I sense the knights will soon need my help. (Matthew 4:1-11)

THE ANCIENT OF DAYS YAHWEH GOD, KING OF ETERNITY SPEAKS.

Yes, my son you are correct in your thinking. The knights are in a war of words with our former brother, and now their accuser. Soon you will indeed have to help them. All power in heaven and on earth has been given to you. (Matthew 28:18) It is up to you to decide how you will assist them.

PART 2. THE DRAGON SPEAKS. (BOLD KNIGHT vs. DARK SOUL.)

BOLD KNIGHT:

Dark Soul, you have set loose your dragon of venom and hate
To do battle with you, I can't wait

My body and my mind are both ready and poised
And like Prince Passion, I too, will make you annoyed

But I hope my words will more than annoy
To totally enrage you, is my ploy

Dark Soul . . . no . . . Mouse Heart is what you should be called
Your twisted, thoughtless thinking is absolutely flawed

You scoff and mock our princess and the eternal king too
But it was him that first gave life to you

Ungrateful and inconsiderate you really are
You are now our greatest threat by far

Your words of hate are lower than the dirt
But they just bounce off and cause me no hurt

Words like joy, peace, and love, which always is first
These words put into practice, is what you fear worst

Dark Soul, YOU are the true coward and it's love you fear
You changed your heart's color, and won't let love come near

A lonely miserable speck of dust you are in the universe
But when you choose hate over love, you are truly cursed

Cursed because your heart resembles the color of night
Like a scared roach, you turn and run from love's light

A roach you are in another way
For all the vile and cruel things you say

My brother knights and I are not perfect, that's true
We each have our doubts, fears, and feelings of blue

At times, our hearts too are overwhelmed
We then pray to the Most High in heaven's realm

He calms our hearts and soothes our souls
Knowing he is there makes us once again bold

I know I look nothing like the handsome Prince Charming
Some may gaze upon me and find my looks alarming

How could a princess, lovely and pretty
Love someone whose face makes some feel pity

Ridiculed and covered with scars am I
I often wonder too, how I caught her eye

Maybe it was the magnificent King Eternal destined plan
For my lady to be loved by the hands of this man (9)

But this I know ----------------

DARK SOUL INTERRUPTS BOLD KNIGHT

Bold Knight, you have the nerve to call me a roach and a worm
Here is another thing about me you should learn
Your silly words do not make me squirm

For I too, like you knights, am brave and bold
But all this love nonsense is getting very old
Love has many sad stories that should have never been told

Stand down and watch as this "worm"
Turn loose his "dragon" to make YOU tremble and squirm

My words are now directed only to you
You will feel like an ant when I am through

You AND your brother knights can go straight to Hell
That's a place I know all too well

With a name like "Bold" means you are supposed to be brave
But not even a pesky fly you could save

A little lost dog is what you resemble
You don't have enough courage to put into a thimble

The crazy queen, King Eternal, and you are all the same
You all are big fools, with a pea brain
Everything you all say, is just totally lame

Yeah, I just called all three of you dumb, lame and dense
None of you have any common or good sense

You say that love is so right
That's not what I see in my sight

Through the centuries, I've seen love that started the right way
Then it turned into not caring, and went astray

I still see love that began so zealous
Change into something insecure and jealous

Dark Soul with his deadly trazokk and trizokk weapons

At times, two's love gets twisted and mangled
And turns into a corrupt love triangle

I've seen lovers swear an oath of loyalty until death
Only for one to cause, and take the other's last breath

I don't think your supposedly "wise" Eternal King
Was thinking very smart when he created this love thing

I pay no attention to any of love's best
It's worthless to me and I couldn't care less

To me, its love's stupidity and love's worst
That in my dark heart always comes first

Then YOU, Bold Knight, looking the way you do
You're right! How could a queen or any woman EVER love you?

With the face of something that looks like a dog
And you're as dumb as a bump on a log

You deserve every word of my contempt and scorn
How I wish you were never born

I feel I am just wasting my breath on you dumb knights
So just go away now, and get out of my sight!

Go crawl away like a scared snake
So I can again taunt your mud duck princesa and cause her
more heartbreak

BOLD KNIGHT:

No, it's YOU that should slither away like a snake

For all your insults and accusations, I can take

You are nothing more than an insecure, thoughtless fool
Who uses lies and more lies, as his tool

NEVER will I run away, or my brothers either
In this fight Dark Soul you will not get a breather

Our King's glory and honor we will never forsake
And our love for our princess we will never break

You use cruel words to make us feel weak and small
But they have an opposite effect and make us stand more tall

What you say about me is part of your warped, sick plan
Your cruel words make you so much less of a man

OOPS! Sorry. I mistakenly called you a man
You're like something that crawls across the land

Ant, roach, or even a flying mosquito
You need to take your hate, and far away go

The lowest you are in the insect kingdom
The dirt of the Earth is where you also are from

Your deceptive words are like the thing whose tail is a rattle
Now your slippery words have slithered you into one great battle

Dark Soul, you should know that we will never back down
So I hope you're ready for a hard fight, you twisted clown

A twisted clown, because you think it's fun
To make cloudy a heart that loves so bright, like the sun

Ed Hendricks

Yes, my lady has seen love's bad and good
She chose its best, like a true heart should

While she chose love, you choose to hate
Now your heart is in a sad, sorry dark state

You see how love makes her so happy
And that makes your mind sick with jealousy

You then invent this warped harebrained scheme
To shatter her heart and her love dream

Through the ages, there have been many idiots like you
That used malice and envy to break hearts so true

Sometimes you fail and sometimes you succeed
Then it's more bad feelings you help to breed

I too have witnessed love's good and bad
I've seen it also change from happy to sad

I choose to focus on its best
For nothing good comes without first a test

This I know, for I have fought many a fight
To love my lady and make her heart feel right

But you, Dark Soul, whose heart is pitch black and scared yellow
Are just one sad, wretched fellow

Behind all your hate is so much fear
That you won't let an ounce of love come near
Your wicked purpose is now very clear

Maybe if you change your heart from dark to light
That will dissolve all your fright

However, you're so set in your crooked way
Your "dragon" my brothers and I stand ready to slay

So Dark Soul, you need to stop all your mindless bragging
And "fly" far away on your spineless "dragon"

BOLDEYE: WOW! Our brave brother Bold Knight is going toe-to-toe with Dark Soul and is holding his own very well. Dark Soul has unleashed his "dragon" expecting it to cause fear and cowardice in the knights. But instead, it has brought out of them even more dedication and determination. What Dark Soul first thought would be easy has become harder for him to accomplish because of the intrepid knights.

We know that Dark Soul will not give up on his devious plan to sadden forever the heart of their queen and to ridicule the Eternal King. What other malicious intent does he have in mind? Let's return to our feature and see.

More of my angelic brothers have taken great interest in this tale. I am now joined by three legions of the Swift Star Angels, who fly with the Godspeed Cherubim. They carry out our Eternal King's and his faithful son, our Lord Jesus Christ's commands inside the blink of an eye. Some of these loyal brothers appeared to the prophet Ezekiel. (Ezekiel Chapters 1 and 10)

Also with them is one of the mighty Seven Supreme Seraphim, Thunder Hand. We usually see him when a great battle is near or is already being fought. I wonder why he is with us now?

DARK SOUL:

Ed Hendricks

Bold Knight, you are proving to be a pest of a foe
But let me say this now, so that you know

All you speak and then what I choose to hear
Goes in and out so fast of my ear

Your courage and words both are fake
You need to just shut up and go jump in a lake

Also, jump in it with your so-called rat brothers
And also take your rodent fathers and mothers

I want to finally and totally be rid of you all
So if not a lake, then go climb something high, and fall

Either way you choose, just do it now
So I can once again demean your princess sow

Bold Knight . . . no, Knight of Fright
You look like a blind mammal that flies at night

All of you and your king as well
Can join me in the deepest darkest corner of Hell

I couldn't care less about your hideous queen
The most frightening heifer I've ever seen

You fools just don't know what a big mess you're in now
By daring to oppose me and save your ugly cow

I now offer you stupid knights an easy way out
Just turn and run away fast, you fat head lout

This is your only and last chance

To forget this "bravery" stance

You and your lame brain brothers of the light
Can once again get far away from my sight

Oh wait! I just thought of something new
That you misguided knights can do

Why don't you all come join up with me
And forget all that fake bravery

Your hearts will be like mine, with no more light
Not having to pretend anymore to stand for what's right

Like Job's wife, I tell you now to curse your King Eternal (Job 2:9,10)
And come with me in my hate-filled inferno

We'll break many hearts and shatter many minds
We'll do many things that are not kind

We'll spread so much misery among the human race
All while cursing God to his face

To "that son" of his, we will do the same
Like WE who killed him did, calling him many a vile name

I could use you knights in my own dark way
If you come over to my side and stay

As a bonus, I will throw in the world and its riches
So your pockets will no longer be "in the ditches"

For I know you dumb knights are just barely above being poor

Join up with me and that will happen no more

So Bold Knight, what do you say
Will you all come over to my side today?

BOLD KNIGHT:

OH, BUT NO!
To your side we will NEVER go!
You are truly a demented foe

You have absolutely lost your tiny beetle brain
And now have totally gone insane

NEVER will we betray our kings and princess so dear
To you I want to make this very clear

To even ask that idiot question, you have quite the nerve
Oh crooked Dark Soul, you we will never serve

There is a creature I know you can ask that
You and it are the same, for you both are rats

A rat you are, covered in scum
I think the rat is smarter, because you're really dumb

You have called us thick headed and dim of wits
But around your head stupidity now sits

Stupid because you choose hate over love
Its beauty and splendor you now know nothing of

Then our eternal king you dare to curse
When it comes to being ignorant, you're the worst

But there is one thing you are the best at
As I said before, it's being a rat

With the heart of a mouse that you already have
Not my queen, but it's YOU that looks like a calf

There's another beast of the field of which you remind me
Its likeness is that of a donkey

Not only in looks, but also in thought
Your dark heart learned the stubbornness it taught

Wow Dark Soul you are one very odd creature
Worm, rat, roach, calf, and donkey your looks now feature

Add to all this, a mouse heart too
You're like nothing I've ever seen in a zoo

But if you want to change your heart from the color of the night
I will help you to again let love in, and make it shine so bright

You will know so much joy and bliss
Feelings that you will not want to ever again miss

Focus on its good or bad, it's your choice
Whether your heart sings the blues or praises of rejoice

So Dark Soul, I'm giving you one last chance also
To open your heart to love, and let its delightful feeling flow

BOLDEYE: This villain of the heart Dark Soul has defamed not only our eternal king, but Queen Splendina and our earthly brothers, the Knights as well. But Bold Knight still offers to help Dark Soul find love again in his heart. How noble he is! Just like a true knight of days long ago passed. This remarkable courage also flows through all of his brothers too. Will Dark Soul accept his offer to love again?

Let's find out.

Many thousands of angels are now here in the realm of heaven gathered together to watch this tale play out with great interest.

DARK SOUL:

Bold "Not" Knight I give you back the very same NO!
AGAIN, to jump in a deep lake, you should go

You will never get my black heart to again turn
The hottest fires of Hell is where it forever burns

Besides, I LOVE to see the effects of my hate and misery
Have upon the whole of humanity

Because you humans are "that thing" in Heaven special creation
I LOVE to divide you all, nation by nation

Race, color, politics, money, location, religion
I drop hatred on them all, like a "loose" pigeon

These are my favorites, but I use many others
To turn mothers against fathers, sisters against brothers

Remember, I too have been around for a very long time
And I have many "partners" in this crime

Every human weakness I see and find
I use it against love, to undermine

You humans make it so very easy for me
To spread all my dark powers of enmity

I've seen you turn against one another for some of the dumbest reasons
Winter, spring, summer, fall, my destructive work is never out of season

Also, if I have to, I'll pick you humans off one by one
Whenever I turn love to hate, my job is done

However, I always keep in the back of my mind
That I will soon be out of time

For that fool in Heaven will soon send back his son (Revelation 19:11-21)
To undo all of my evil fun

That very same son I tried to kill when he was born
To cause his father's heart grief and make it mourn

It was I, who *helped* to move that star (Matthew 2:9)
That showed the wise men (astrologers) where they (Joseph, Mary, and the baby Jesus) are (Matthew 2:1-12)

I even used King Herod to try to kill him as a baby (Matthew 2:7, 13-16)
But my former brother was sent from Heaven to tell them to flee (Matthew 2:13)

Thirty-three years later, I helped to succeed in his son's death (Matthew Chapters 26 and 27, verses 1-54)
I too, was three inches from his face when he took his last Earth breath (Note: This was Jesus *before* his resurrection)

Ed Hendricks

I was cursing him to his face while he hung on the cross
Telling him in this world, I'm also the boss

My darker purpose was to break his love for woman and man
That also was my sinister plan

To make him betray heaven and humanity, so he would totally fail
And join me in the darkest part of Hell

But "that son" of his died faithful and loyal
And now he stands at the right side of Heaven's throne, grand and royal

So the same tricks I tried to use on him
I try and succeed with you humans, again and again

However, with you pesky knights, I've run into a roadblock
How many more things about you can I mock?

You just WILL NOT GO AWAY! And I'm getting very mad
If you don't leave now, you soon wish you had

BOLD KNIGHT:

OH! So more of your dastardly purposes are now coming out
Of your twisted, tortured, terribly evil mouth

Your rat face has been here since very long ago
I was beginning to suspect that, but now I know

From the devil himself you have been sent
Not only is your horridly cruel and wicked mind twisted, it is totally bent!

You and your master have wreaked much havoc upon the human race
To love itself you have tried to lay waste

Throughout the ages, you have caused humanity to groan and wail
But today my brothers and I will gladly send you back to Hell

Our kings and our queen we will never leave
About us, their hearts will never grieve

Dark Soul, you speak with the mind of a rat, and the tongue of a snake
It's YOU that needs to go jump in a very deep lake

But soon you and your evil master will be thrown into the lake of fire (Revelation 20:10)
By the Most High in heaven's son whom we call "sire"

A hater, liar, and tyrant you are, all rolled into one
To see you burn forever, now THAT would be humanity's fun

With you will burn all of your hate
When you helped to have King Eternal's son murdered, you sealed your fate

For now, Worm Soul, we are still here
Standing up to your vicious accusations and fear

I told you earlier -------

The Century Princess gently interrupts Bold Knight

My dear Bold Knight, please may I now speak

For I too have heard all of Dark Soul's lies and accusations
His half-truths, taunts, and insults
However you, my brave and trusted champion Bold Knight
Have courageously stood up and defended our king's glory
And my honor too
Your brother knights have joined you in this grand quest
Protecting our king, his son and myself
For your uncommon valor, WE are eternally grateful
WE being every woman who has ever loved deeply
And still does today
And wants to forever

I must first apologize to my steadfast knights
Who zealously guard my heart
And leaped to my aid against this madman
I foolishly let his cruel words infect my happiness
Destroy my joy

Like you bold warriors, I sometimes am down in spirit
Faint of heart
Worrisome in mind
My stress is great as well
My faith falters

I let Dark Soul's horrible words stay inside me too long
And they caused me much sadness

I have witnessed the worst of love through the centuries too
How it started so right and ended so wrong
How is was first blessed, then time cursed
How it began in truth, but ended in lies
How it enriched life and caused death

Into a bottomless pit my heart entered

I could smell its dank odor
Feel its ominous presence surround me
I sensed my doom was near

I would have stayed there if it were not for my intrepid knights
My personal champions of the heart

Each of you have defended me in separate ways
As you have done in the past and still do today
But you all come out as equal
Equal in bravery, determination
Loyalty (10)

My outspoken warrior leader, Bold Knight
Who withstood Dark Soul's "dragon"
You took the most of his abuse
Then dished out some of your own in kind
He mocked, ranted, threatened so much
Yet your courage was unwavering
Never once did you back down
Even when his so-called "dragon" tempted you personally
You remained loyal to our king and his son
And myself

Just like our king's prophet of old, Elijah
He and you both were taunted and threatened by true evil
(1 Kings Chapter 18)
But you both remained loyal under fire
Impressed I am greatly of you
A dedicated leader you truly are

My noble Brave Duke
Just as brave as your younger brother, Bold Knight
And just as faithful

To answer Dark Soul's vile words
With strength of character
Resolve of faith

To not give in to his contempt
Proves your allegiance to the ones in the heavens too
Blessed I am to have you for a protector

To my adoring Richard the Deep Hearted
Whose love is boundless
And whose courage is the same

Your endless love for me fills my heart with happiness
My soul leaps with joy
My spirit dances with delight
For me to know and feel your tender love
As well as your faith and fortitude
A grateful thanks to you I graciously give

Lest I not forget you too, my devoted Sir Romance A Lot
Who worships his king wholeheartedly
And loves me the same

Together with your knight brothers, you helped to "slay" Dark
Soul's feeble dragon
Turning it into a powerless worm
With complete and great admiration, I thank you so very much
for your solid dedication

Lastly, yet lovingly, to you my loyal lover Prince Passion
Who first loves my mind
Then makes such sweet love to my body
To the stars and beyond you always take me too
Over and over again

KNIGHTS OF BRAVELOVE

Though you are attentive to my mind, then body
You have also vowed to serve our king
And protect my honor

Dark Soul has also accused you of cowardice
Tempted you with treason against heaven
Even offering you the riches of this world
In his own deceptive way

With your brothers, you have proved him to be a liar
A fraud, an apostate

So happy you have made my heart because of your dedication
Eternally grateful I am for you as well

My Knights,
Oh my brave and beloved knights
So much respect I have for our king and his son
And for each of you as well

I have been blessed throughout time
With the love of and from our creator
And with the love of and from my knights

My heart once again sings the praises of love
Feel its joy and its beauty
My spirit glides upon its wings
Soars so free above the clouds

I can answer your repulsive sarcasm Dark Soul
Your hateful and hideous taunts
In full faith, I now can tell you
That I stand in complete unison with my knights
Impressed so much I am of their true, raw courage

I am so proud of their fierce loyalty to our king
And to my heart

Dark Soul . . . no, Ant Soul, you can go back to your evil master
And tell him you have failed
Both you and he are total losers
You both have been for ages
And soon will be forever

BOLD EYE, THE ARCHANGEL OF THE CHERUBIM: YES!
The Century Princess has regained her honor and her heart is
once again joyful and happy. Our earthly brothers, the Knights,
have taken the full force of a cruel, vicious, attack of words by
Dark Soul and his "dragon" and proceeded to "slay" it. The
intrepid Bold Knight has lived up to his name once more and
shown true valor by taking the largest part of Dark Soul's
slanderous words and never backing down.

Those of us in heaven witnessing this epic odyssey of the heart
are greatly impressed with the fortitude of our heroes of the
heart. Even the mighty seraphim Thunder Hand have expressed
his admiration too. You humans know of his power for it was
him who had to punish your King David for his disobedience in
taking an illegal census. (2 Samuel 24:1-17)

Very curious we all are to know what the imagination of King
Eternal's humble poet reveals next. Let's eagerly read on and
find out.

BOLD KNIGHT:

Dark Soul, you have failed in your cowardly attempt
To forever make our captivating lady and all women sad, with
your scorn and contempt

"My heart again sings the praises of love" is what she just said
Our loyalty to our king and her has slain your weak "dragon" dead

As I stated before to you, we will NEVER give in
We thank God and his son Christ, for this hard earned win

Go and take this message back to the evil one you serve
Tell him he sent a spineless, wimpy dragon that has no nerve

Now, go far away and leave us be
So we can give thanks and praise to our King of Eternity

RICHARD THE DEEP HEARTED:

It's I again, Richard the Deep Hearted
Still here watching, listening
Taking in all this mess Dark Soul has started

I wonder how much of an idiot you really are
Hurling insults at our kings and princess
YOU are the biggest fool here, by far

For you choose to love again never
Missing out on its beauty and splendor
That does not make you look very clever

Your hate has turned you into something twisted and sick
A counterfeit treacherous weasel
Your choice of the dark side, you did pick

Look at you now, vile and rude
Your place among the lowest creatures assured
All because of your worse-than-bad attitude

Unlike you, my brave brothers and I choose love's best
Never easy it was, and today still isn't
But time and time again, we passed test after test

Tried, tested and still remaining true
Displaying exceptional courage
Again, isn't that what we that love deeply do?

Even to this very minute of time and space
I love my adorable lady whole-hearted
An everlasting feeling that your hate will not replace

So, Weasel Soul, Bold Knight is whom I faithfully stand with
In every word he speaks
Between him and me there is no rift

Hurry back to your deceptive master very fast
And tell him all our words
From the hottest fires of Hell, he will punish your failure with a blast

And as you feel your wicked master's wrath
Causing you much pain and torment
Remember, it was we knights that caused it by blocking your devious path

SIR ROMANCE A LOT:

To the one whose soul is the color of night
And whose heart has no light
Who tried to put our Lady Love's heart in everlasting plight
Then tried to turn us knights away with dread and fright

Many wrongs you and your "dragon" spoke

It huffed and puffed and blew much smoke
But our resolute commitment turned it into a joke

So funny it looks now, and at you we laugh
No longer a dragon, but more like a newborn calf
Weak and defenseless, its size now less than half

You have lost this hand of your distorted, counterfeit game
Mouse Soul, the pathetic loser is your new name
For you and failure are one and the same

You are also a bully and a liar
That dwells with the lowest creatures living in the mire
Don't you have anything better to aspire?

To the ones in the heavens that we call sire
To our princess whose love lifts our hearts and spirits higher
These are the ones who sets our valor on fire

For true love and true courage never grow old
They are the greatest stories ever told
An inspiration for all to be fearless and bold

Isn't this is what deep love should be?
A shining example for humanity
That is what we knights pray for unceasingly

So Dark . . . no, Chicken Wing Soul, I too agree with what my brothers have said
Let this go deep inside your thoughtless, thick head
You and your toothless "dragon" caused us no fear or dread
This false "technique" of yours, you need to shed
Between us, your senseless hate will never spread
We think there is something better you can now do instead

That is to go away now and just drop dead!

PRINCE PASSION:

In total agreement I am with my beloved, sensuous Sultana
Who radiates and attracts dreamy desire
Whom I also love with all my heart
My audacious brother knights, I stand firmly with too

We have taken so much abuse from this fiendish coward
His heart and mind are the same color as his name
He wants to infect all true lovers and all like them
By spreading his cruel thoughts to all of humanity

Contempt and ridicule reign supreme in HIS batty brain
Bat headed Dark Soul with a bat brain? Hmmm . . .

To reject love is to reject life
For love is life's sweetest reward
An infinite blessing from The Lord above
I always remember this in every kiss
In every tender touch and caress
Of my beloved one

Dark Soul . . . no, Buzzard Soul
I absolutely stand in total unison with my brothers
To first love and honor our King Eternal
Then our splendid queen

Return to that mirror you call a master
A mirror because you both look like jackasses now
Also because your twisted, corrupt scheme has totally failed!

DARK SOUL ROARS LOUDLY WITH GREAT ANGER:

YOU STUPID FOOLS! IDIOTS!

YOU HAVE MADE MY ANGER BOIL OVER!
IT NOW ERUPTS LIKE AN ANGRY VOLCANO

I warned you before I was getting mad
But none of you dimwit knights chose to listen
I almost succeeded in forever turning your hen princess's heart sad
Her grief was such sweet music to my ears
Her pain soothed the darkest part of my soul
Throughout time itself I mastered this intimidation
Perfected it

It usually works to my wicked delight
Sometimes it does not
That is when I unleash my dragon
To dismay, disappoint, and cause much distress

But you half-a-brain knights have interfered with my evil intentions toward your pig princess
Now she is made happy once again

SO FURIOUS I AM WITH YOU ALL!

For me to get to her once again, I have to go through you knights
Well, I am FINE with that

JUST FINE!

For my time is short before Judgment Day

You defied all my warnings to leave

You knights wanted a fight? Well now you have one

YOUR LAST ONE!

TODAY, I WILL KILL ALL OF YOU!!!

Death's final call will soon be in your ears
Me taking your lives today is now all your fears

Interfere with my plans you have done
I will soon make sure you never see another sun

Very soon, you knights will surely fall
At last your ears will answer Death's call

Each of you so-called knights I will slay
This is how I will permanently make you go away

Then I will again attack your slimy eel princess
So too, I will break all women like her in spirit
Since you all will soon join me in Hell
Reveal myself to you I will
I am second in command of ALL the demon hordes
Second only because I left Heaven right after my master
The devil himself

Ready yourselves you misfit knights
My wrath you will soon feel, and be destroyed by
Return to my master I will not, before having spilled your blood

BOLDEYE THE ARCHANGEL: WOW! Dark Soul now reveals his true identity and nature. Who he is and who really sent him. But even worse, he has sworn to kill our fearless earthly brothers, the Knights of Brave Love, and to once again turn his dragon loose upon and all women who want to give and receive love truly and deeply

The human knights are no match whatsoever for Dark Soul, who also has revealed himself to be second in command of all the demon hordes. We here in heaven suspected where he came from, but now we know for sure that he is pure evil. As this war of words escalated with the knights, his evil intent became more and more clear. Now there is no doubt what his dastardly plans are. No doubt at all.

Grave danger now awaits them and at the cost of losing their lives to this evil villain of the heart. The knights have faced many a foe before and mostly come off victorious. Even after a loss, they have remained loyal and faithful to the King of Eternity and his noble son. But they have never faced an adversary as strong as this Dark Soul.

Around me there is great excitement in the air and much animated talk. All my angelic brothers have their own opinions and ideas as to what will happen next. My brothers are asking me so many questions. I have to tell them to be patient and let's see what King Eternal's meek poet reveals to us next.

BOLD KNIGHT:

My brothers,
All my brave, firm-in-faith brothers
Listen to my words carefully
This rat fiend Dark Soul has finally revealed who and what he really is and his horrible intentions towards us
He has used much scorn and contempt against our eternal king and his everlasting son
And our lovely princess he has mocked with glee

Now he seeks our demise for interfering with his evil plans
A death sentence he has issued for our very lives
Our doom is in his warped sights

Throughout time, we have fought against many evils. Most battles we have won, but some we have lost
Our kings and princess we have made proud no matter the outcome

Today I seek their same respect
For it's their glory that deserves our utmost bravery and dedication
This is the least we can do to prove our love for them

My stalwart fellow knights,
Great is the danger that we are about to face
Our very lives are to be taken from us
By this madman, this apostate
THIS LOSER!

Should any of you choose to not stand with me to maintain our king's honour
I will understand if you leave me be
To accept my fate from this evil toad Dark Soul
I pray we will be united again in the resurrection (Revelation 2:6 and 20:4-6)

BRAVE DUKE:

My younger audacious brother
Like you, I refuse to back down
From this reckless and stupid clown
No fear whatsoever I have of him
And the wicked one he serves

To our kings and queen I will remain true
No matter what Dark Soul threatens to do
A fight to the death awaits me too!

PRINCE PASSION:

Add me to this magnificent quest, my brave brothers
Like yourselves, our kings' glory and the love for our princess is
more than worth fighting over
And dying for
Let's show this vulture face Dark Soul what real courage is
For he obviously lacks it

SIR ROMANCE A LOT:

Add one more to go against this jackass Dark Soul
Who not only resembles a rat, but also a mole

Side-by-side, battling together
We will uphold our king's sovereignty forever

I too, am with you until the end
For I am a true and loyal friend

RICHARD THE DEEP HEARTED:

There is love and then there's war
Sometimes you have to go to war for love
Win or lose my brothers, I am with you

DARK SOUL:

Loser? Clown? Vulture? Jackass? Mole?
You foolish knights dare again to mock me when your doom is

so very near?
This is another reason why I called you stupid earlier
Ready yourselves to feel the wrath of this "Loser"

BOLD KNIGHT:

We know who you really are and your true evil intent
If today we are to die by your monkey paw hand, then so be it

But all of heaven will know that we willfully give our lives for the majesty of our king and his faithful and true son. And our beloved princess. Never will our integrity or audacity be questioned by anyone. Especially by you and those like you in your evil spirit world and in the world where we humans dwell.

Gather around me now my brothers, and let us speak our last words to El-Elyon (The Most High God)

THE PRAYER OF BOLD KNIGHT

Sovereign Lord of all the universes, Yahweh God, It is I, your loyal servant Bold Knight, along with my valiant brothers Brave Duke, Sir Romance A Lot, Richard The Deep Hearted, and Prince Passion.

Before your magnificent throne we stand today to first praise your glory and to exalt your greatness. You are more than worthy of the highest honor all of creation can give you. It is by your great hands, working with your fathomless and boundless mind that all things exist.

Celestial Father, we humbly come before you to plead for courage beyond what is normal. The same courage you gave our Lord and your determined son Christ, when he was on the cross sacrificing his life for all of humanity. Like Christ, we pray to uphold your magnificence against the vile, cruel accusations and lies of this evil Dark Soul, and his very wicked master, the devil himself.

Today, he has sworn to destroy us and to once again attack the heart of our precious princess. It is his treacherous plan to spread the darkness in his soul to the hearts of every woman.

El Shaddai (God Almighty), we pray for your wisdom and power to help us stop this wicked plan of his. And should this noble quest cost our lives, we pray that you send others to continue this fight with the same valor your great hand blessed Christ and us with.

With the utmost of respect and humility, I present this prayer to our Lord and Savior Jesus Christ. For no one comes to you except through him. (John 14:6) May he find favor with this lowly prayer from his sincere servants. In the name of Jesus Christ we earnestly pray.

Amen

UNKNOWN TO HER KNIGHTS, THE CENTURY PRINCESS HAS SAID A PRAYER OF HER OWN

My great and immortal king, wonderful and outstanding Yahweh God, may your glory stand to time indefinite upon time indefinite. May all your good works great and small do the same.

El Elyon, (The Most High God) you have blessed me with the protectors of my heart, The Knights of Brave Love. Many times throughout time, they have answered my call of distress. But now, oh Universal Sovereign Lord, my defenders are in severe mortal danger by this crazed Dark Soul, who seeks their ruin. I beg of your highness to please allow me to pray for them and to help them in a way that your infinite wisdom knows is best. With all my heart and all my soul, I plead in earnest to you, my Eternal King.

In the name and power of your obedient son, our Lord Jesus Christ, I pray for your understanding and justice.

Amen

PART 3. UNIVERSAL WAR. (HEAVEN VS. HELL) THE BATTLE FOR BRAVE LOVE.

IN THE GREAT THRONE ROOM OF HEAVEN, THE GLORIOUS LORD JESUS CHRIST SPEAKS WITH URGENCY.

Abba (Father), our loyal servants the fearless knights are indeed in terrible danger from this diabolical Dark Soul. Doing nothing to help them will surely spell their doom. There is MUCH more at stake here to let Dark Soul's sinister purpose manifest. I will send the Supreme Seraphim Truth Sword to protect the knights from Dark Soul.

YAHWEH GOD, SOVEREIGN LORD OF ALL SPEAKS:

Yes, send Truth Sword to help the knights against Dark Soul's treachery. Also have the Supreme Seraphim Brave Fire go with him for added strength. We both know how this demon works. We are well aware of the wicked nature of this tyrant. And of the tricks he will attempt to use against them.

DARK SOUL:

Ready yourselves, you stupid knights, for your moment of death is now here
Once you're all gone, I will spread more hate and fear

I will start with the heart of that queen heifer
Then I will spread my poison to the heart of every woman forever

To corrupt then destroy ALL love through time

Is the ultimate goal in this twisted scheme of mine

Then I will ----------

TRUTH SWORD INTERRUPTS DARK SOUL:

You will do no such thing Dark Soul. The son of our King Eternal has sent me and my angelic brother Brave Fire to guard the knights from your evil plan to kill them. I have also been given the authority to reveal to the knights myself and my brother Brave Fire. And to also reveal you to them as well. My lord sends a message to you Dark Soul to cease your cruel and devious plan, and to return back to your master to await the soon-to-be Day of Judgment.

DARK SOUL:

I will NEVER cease my hostility against heaven or humanity and until the judgment day occurs, WAR IS ON! Once we were brothers, Truth Sword. But now we are sworn enemies in complete opposites of purpose. You and Brave Fire can go back to "that thing" in heaven and tell him to stay out of my affairs. This is my business and--------

BRAVE DUKE INTERRUPTS DARK SOUL:

Dark Soul, we now see you in all your foulness. Though you resemble an angel, all over you are black. From the top of your twisted head to your bent crow feet, it all resembles the abyss that you and your evil master and demon hordes will soon be a part of. (Revelation 20:1-3) Even your wings are the color of the darkest night. We have only heard your voice up to this moment, but now we all see what and who you really are. I never knew that demons and rats looked alike. But seeing you, now I know---------

DARK SOUL YELLS AT BRAVE DUKE:

SHUT UP BRAVE DUKE, YOU IMBECILE! Just because Truth Sword and Brave Fire are here does not mean I will not kill you and your idiotic knight brothers. My plan for your destruction and for as much of humanity as possible before my own demise still exists, and still is in full effect since I first left heaven many centuries ago. This little interference by these disloyal ex-brothers of mine is just a minor distraction from my present purpose. Let this be known: I am going to slay you empty brained knights one way or another.

RICHARD THE DEEP HEARTED:

I speak for all of my brothers who are with me today. Truth Sword and Brave Fire, my angelic comrades, all praise and glory be to the ones we serve. Our King Eternal and his faithful and true son, the Lord Christ. May their greatness stand forever upon forever.

My brother angels of truth, we thank you so very, very much for your unwavering service to our king and his son. We are much honored and blessed to have you here today to protect us from this maniac Dark Soul, who seeks our ruin and to again ruin the heart of our dear princess. If our king chose not to send both of you, we would have gladly given our lives for his glory and his great name. May he remember our deeds and our commitment to him in the coming resurrections. (Revelation 20:4-6 and verses 11-13)

PRINCE PASSION: (WITH MUCH DETERMINATION, YET REMAINING HUMBLE.)

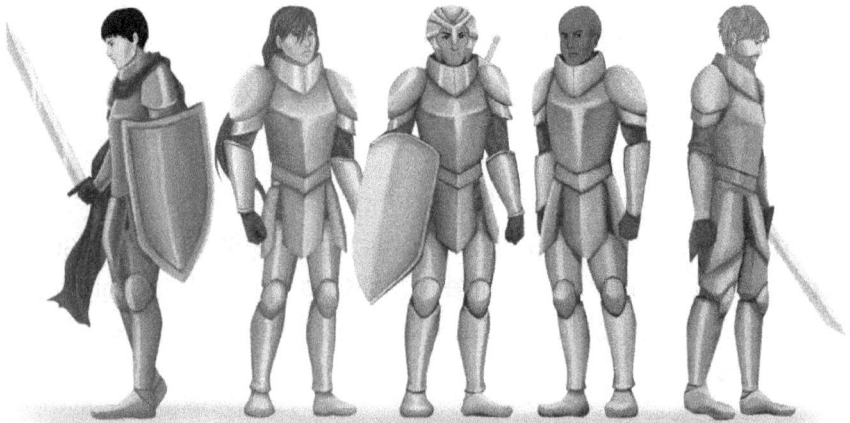

| Richard the Deep Hearted | Prince Passion | Bold Knight | Brave Duke | Sir Romance A Lot |

The Knights of Brave Love

I too, speak for my brother knights by saying that we are true knights that have had to fight many hard battles, visible and invisible. This day, we face a foe that we first did not see, but just heard. Now because of our king's wisdom, he has chosen to reveal this profane enemy to us. We knew from his crooked words that he was evil. Now his rotten darkness has been revealed. My angelic brothers, may our king's power be with all of us, this day and every day. May he bless us with the extraordinary courage to face whatever this lizard brain Dark Soul may throw our way. In the name of The Lord Christ, I ask for strength beyond what is normal to uphold the sovereignty of Heaven.

BOLD EYE THE ARCHANGEL: I am in the middle of a great crowd of my fellow angels, and all of them are talking with great excitement about what is happening. The Lord Christ has sent two of the Seven Supreme Seraphim to guard the knights from Dark Soul's wicked, murderous intent. A third Supreme Seraphim, Thunder Hand, has been with us and he too is talking very excited and loud.

The knights can see Dark Soul and know for sure that they have help from Heaven to stand up against this evil apostate. Even without help from above, they swore to die valiantly and loyal to King Eternal.

All of heaven is now very, very eager to see what events happen next.

DARK SOUL: (WITH MUCH MALICE AND CONTEMPT)

Truth Sword and Brave Fire, the two of you are strong enough to stop me alone from killing these stupid, half-wit knights. Since there are two of you and only one of me, maybe I should call on some more help too. I now summon the demon Asmodai and his foul hordes of followers. They will deal with you two while I finish off these moron knights.

BOLD EYE: As I am listening with great interest to this exchange, I suddenly see a large horde of my former brothers, now sworn enemies, gather behind Dark Soul. With them are their dark swords, spears, battle-axes, bow and arrows and shields of all shapes and sizes by their sides.

I recognize Jystrox and Taladrog, the main ones who opposed my faithful brother Gold Wing who was sent to give a message to the prophet Daniel, but had to call on the mighty archangel Michael for help to get our king's message through. (See Daniel 10:13 and also verses 20, 21)

I also see my former friend Bletarz, who permanently left heaven and is now allied with Dark Soul and his cruel master. They now number into the hundreds of thousands and their sinister purpose is the same as their leader. I look at Bletarz now and I am saddened. Thinking back when we were together serving under our kings. That day of fun we had racing each other through the Kmatulaan Galaxy.

These former brothers lost their heavenly names that were blessed upon them by the Lord Christ when they chose to follow their rebellious leaders and leave heaven permanently. They now have the unholy names that their vile master the devil has given them instead.

Even more excited are the voices of the hosts of heaven after this. There is anticipation in the air of the immense clash that is about to occur. A continuation of the many battles both angels and humans have already fought, and still are fighting today.

THE DEMON ASMODAI SPEAKS:

My filthy brother Dark Soul, I have heard your call and now am here to answer it. I bring with me my fiendish soldiers, the 13 Hordes of the Necronomus Abysmal from Hell. We are here to help you in any way with your evil purpose. We also have heard the words of these misfit knights and now we see that Truth Sword and Brave Fire are here to stop you. My dark, depraved brother, we join with you to oppose them and their king.

THE LORD JESUS CHRIST:

I will send forth the Supreme Seraphim's Thunder Hand and Great Arm to stand with Truth Sword and Brave Fire. With them will be the legions of angels under their command. Go, my friends and stand firm with your brothers.

BOLD EYE: I am surrounded by so much excited talk and frantic words. Suddenly I see my brother Thunder Hand fly down to be with Truth Sword and Brave Fire. My brother Brave Fire is the angel that protected the three friends of the prophet Daniel from burning to death in King Nebuchadnezzar's fiery furnace. (Daniel Chapter 3) Following him are the Dreadnaught Warriors. And look! I also see the Angels of the Stellar Star Swords and the Starlight Strikers, mighty brothers who fought with me at the Qyyus Galaxy* and later in wars that The Philippines, Argentina, Brazil, and Spain fought in. Let me not forget the Battle of Midway in your human World War II.

The Angels of the Stellar Star Swords and The Starlight Strikers carry swords with them that resemble the light from the stars themselves. In their left hands are shiny, glowing shields made from the Thartazian Octonova, which occurred billions of millenniums ago. This celestial event was so powerful that it destroyed almost all of the Qastarixian Universe. Our King and illustrious Grand Creator had to rebuild it again. (An Octonova is a supernova that is at least eight times more powerful than a normal supernova.)

* The Qyyus Galaxy incident happened because the Evil Ones wanted to move Earth to this far, far away place, thus destroying all life on the planet. When God said no, they then wanted to merge the Qyyus Galaxy into this universe. My brothers were sent there to stop them and after a very hard-fought battle, they were defeated.

THE SUPREME SERAPHIM THUNDER HAND SPEAKS:

Dark Soul, you dare to oppose our king and heaven itself, the very place you used to abide? Then you insist on defaming our Century Princess, and to kill her knights. You are stark, raving mad. Today I join with Truth Sword, Brave Fire, Great Arm and the other loyal armies of heaven to stop your evil plans. The Lord Christ has instructed me to warn you again to stop this rebellion. You will soon face one of your final judgments at the battle of Armageddon. But for now, you must cease this!

DARK SOUL: (WITH DISDAIN AND SCORN)

Once again, my former friend I will NOT stop or back down from my desire to kill these mud-for-brains knights. Just because that rooster king of yours has called on you angels to help them does not mean I will stop. If I have to go through you to get to them, then I will. For now, their demise is my primary goal.

Heaven may have its armies, but I have my dark soldiers too that left heaven after my master and myself. How about I call up some more of them just for fun.

From the Dytharus Pit of Hell, I summon the entire black horde under the command of my very evil brother Wazlarx. I also call to my aid all the demon hordes that control the northern and southern regions of the Earth. And their leaders Molech and Chemosh. Just for even more fun, come join me from the Satazarous foul cave, the Tartummus hordes and from the Quemtarian darkness, the most cruel and vile Varkinian monsters. And their very wicked leader Clydrok.

BOLD EYE: As I see and hear all of this play out, a grand battle is shaping up. On one side are the Armies of Heaven, my angelic brothers clothed in pure white linen robes. Each has a golden sword with them that shines bright like the sun. Only the Angels of the Star Swords and the Starlight Strikers all have glowing swords that resemble the color of the stars. Their leader Great Arm has made his presence known with his mighty sword that was made from the Idaxtum Pulsar. Great Arm is the strong angel mentioned in your bible book of Revelation, chapter 10.

He stands beside his fellow Supreme Seraphim's Thunder Hand, Brave Fire, and Truth Sword. Behind them are the Dreadnaught Warriors, whose courage and fearlessness are known to both angels and demons alike. Four of the Seven Supreme Seraphim and the legions of battle angels under their command are now all gathered together.

On the other side is the psychotic Dark Soul and his demonic hordes. He has called forth Chemosh and Molech, who reign over the northern and southern parts of the Earth. Everything about them is dark. Dark clothes, dark swords, dark intent. He has called up from Hell, Asmodai, Wazlarx, the demons from the Satazorous Cave, The Tartummus hordes, and the Quemtarian Darkness Varkinian horde with their most foul leader, Clydrok.

The air and the ground are filled with angels and demons of all shapes and sizes, but just of very few colors. This reminds me of the black and white that your planet first was before our King Eternal made all things colorful.

Standing next to my brother Brave Fire is the audacious leader of the knights, Bold Knight. Next to him on his right are his loyal brothers Brave Duke, Richard the Deep Hearted, then Sir Romance A Lot, and lastly, Prince Passion. With the ability to now see what and who is around them, the knights have a look of steady determination and focus to fight for their kings and their queen.

DARK SOUL: (WITH A VERY EVIL SMILE ON HIS FACE)

Why should I just stop with only these wicked brothers of mine? I now call up from Hell, the Archduke of the Bratoxzumus Void, Necotor and his filthy followers the Chenarax. From the Latarzus depths, the evil Dratox. And the TRUE master of the Eastern hemisphere of the Earth, Zaltaxus. Follow me, my vile brothers as we go against these bogus knights and those weasels from heaven that supports them. We have nothing to lose before the Day of Judgment, so LET'S DO THIS!

THE KING OF KINGS AND LORD OF LORDS, JESUS CHRIST:

Abba (Father), This Dark Soul has summoned many hordes of demons from both the Earth and the darkest corners of Hell itself. Our brothers are outnumbered 5 to 1. I will send the Archangels Fierce Blade and Courage Strike to match this army of Dark Soul's. With them will go the 12 War Blade Legions under their command. I also will keep the Archangel Michael at ready.

THE SOVEREIGN LORD OF ALL, ELOHIM GOD:

I agree with all you have done in this matter. We must show Dark Soul that he will not succeed in his folly. I now will empower the knights with the strength needed to successfully fight against Dark Soul and his wicked followers.

CHRIST ASKS: Abba, do you think it is wise to grant the knights such incredible powers? They are just only human.

ELOHIM GOD: I am he who examines the hearts and minds of all living things. (1 Chronicles 28:9, Psalms 26:2 and 139:23) These knights have proven throughout time to be of extraordinary courage and bold faith. Even now when I gaze deeply into their hearts as they face great and grave danger, they let their love and honor for me rule in place over their fear. And their love for their princess rule over their plight.

BOLD EYE: I now see my former brothers, now sworn enemies merge into the demonic horde army. From the darkest parts of Hell they come from. The Bratoxzumas Void, The Latarzus Depths, The Dytharus Pit, The Necronomus Abysmal come some of the most evil and wicked of Dark Soul's army. And from the northern, eastern, and southern regions of the Earth come its true rulers and the very wicked followers that lead them.

Suddenly I hear a familiar sound that I have heard countless times before through the centuries. The sound of many thousands of my brothers leaving heaven. In an instant I see Fierce Blade, Courage Strike and the 12 War Blade Legions join the four Supreme Seraphim. Flying behind them are the Angels of the Furious Swords, who are heaven's most skilled and capable warriors. They also helped to defeat Clydrok and his Varkinian horde at the unusual battle of the Spectoxulus

Quasar. And later also stopped Asmodai and his 13 Hordes of the Necronomus Abysmal at your human American Civil War and the Six Day War that Israel fought.

(The Spectoxulus Quasar battle happened when the evil Clydrok and his demonic followers wanted to make the energy from this space phenomenon a part of Hell, thus making it more larger and hotter. So they went to it and tried to bring parts of it back with them. We were sent to stop them from this crazy plan of theirs and another intense battle was fought. They were defeated by Fierce Blade, Courage Strike and the Angels of the Furious Swords and sent back to Hell, humiliated.)

Dark Soul has amassed his evil hordes just to destroy the knights, who have opposed his plan to sadden and disrupt the joy of The Century Princess and for all women. He has gone through a lot of work just for this purpose. This shows the selfish, hateful, I-don't-care attitude of Dark Soul's character.

Old rivalries, old scores that have persisted for ages have come up and are once again being fought over. I gaze down upon the battlefield of the great plain of Megiddo and see former friends now swear an oath of pain and revenge against my true brothers. These sworn enemies are now not only eyeing each other, but positioning their legions and their hordes in battle formations, so that they can confront each other more easily and continue their personal vendettas of the centuries. ALL of heaven is now on full, high alert in anticipation of the titanic clash that is about to happen. Every one of my angelic brothers is ready, myself included, to go to war. Suddenly I see a bright, glowing light emit from the magnificent throne room of heaven.

I recognize it as The Holy Spirit. He touches each of the knights for but a moment, but in that short moment, they shine so very bright. Then the light fades and goes away. The appearances of the knights have changed very much. Instead of being dressed in their meager and very ragged clothing with old battered swords and shields, they now resemble me and my angelic brothers. Dressed in fine shiny armor with gleaming new, long swords and shields.

I stare in fascination of these earthly brothers and can remember many times in the past when our king empowered those whom he found favor with and faced terrible danger. The Nation of Israel from days of old. Moses. Joshua. Your King David. The Prophet Elijah, which many of us in heaven and The Century Princess compare Bold Knight to. Daniel and many others that have inspired you humans from your bibles.

DARK SOUL: (WITH MUCH ARROGANCE IN HIS VOICE)

Well . . . well! I see those I once served side-by-side with I now have to fight against once again. I remember the Qyyus Galaxy incident and the Battle of the Bulge in World War II. The ONLY reason why heaven won that battle was because Michael the Archangel was called into the fray. Otherwise I would have won that AND the Otorzao universe war. My, my, my . . . how time and a rebellion changes things. That king of yours is calling out the heavy hitters of heaven. But all of you still will not stop me from my insidious purpose to slay these idiot, insect brained knights. They picked this fight and even when I warned them to leave, they wouldn't listen. Now they will pay for their fake so-called bravery with their very lives. I will take their last breath from them and give it to my master, Satan the Devil. They kicked Hell's hornet's nest and now have let loose a lot of angry little demons. These wimpy knights don't care about anyone but themselves. They use your reptile King eternal for their own selfish purposes and he is too dumb to realize this. But I---------

RICHARD THE DEEP HEARTED INTERRUPTS DARK SOUL:

You are a stark, raving mad lunatic! All that comes from your filthy, rat faced, jackassed mouth is lies, lies, and more lies. You are just like your evil master, The Devil. The father and inventor of the very first lie ever told.

My insightful brother Bold Knight has already told you that we are fully prepared to do battle with you and your hordes of hellish demons to uphold our king's greatness and our queen's love. As the song "The Impossible Dream"(18) tells, we will fight you, oh vile Dark Soul, The Unbeatable Foe. We will right this unrightable wrong you have made happen. This quest of ours is to follow the stars in the magnificent throne room of heaven. To fight for the causes of sovereignty and honor for our king and to march against and into Hell for this heavenly cause. And should we die true to this glorious quest, we know our hearts will rest in peace and calm because we fought bravely and faithfully against evil of all kinds.

You have scorned heaven, and you have given verbal scars to the names of the ones who rule from its great throne room. Despite all this, we are still here today about to go to war against the wicked forces of Hell.

SIR ROMANCE A LOT:

My brother Richard the Deep Hearted's comparison of the song "The Impossible Dream" is touching, yet so very accurate. We WILL right this unrightable wrong you have started and now seek to prevent from spreading throughout all of humanity. We soon will battle against the dark forces of Hell to make right what you seek to corrupt. Dark Soul, you evil fiend, never will we allow your hate or ANY hate to take over the world without a

Brave Fire

Truth Sword   Thunder Hand   Great Arm

Four of the Seven Supreme Seraphim

hard fight. So prepare yourself and your hordes for ALL OUT WAR!

PRINCE PASSION:

I am in total agreement with what my brothers just spoke. Dark Soul, you are a crazed, mad dog that has to be stopped at all costs. Your hate for heaven and our beloved princess has spread to all life as a whole. Such hate is a vessel that poisons whatever holds it and accepts it as truth. That is your twisted quest, to spread enmity into the world and to cause confusion, sadness, fear and ultimately death. It is our noble quest to stop you and to uphold our king's glory and to show that love conquers all evil. This we have sworn an oath to and if it means war to do so, then so be it. LET'S DO BATTLE! I AM ALL IN!

BRAVE DUKE:

I am on the same side with heaven and with my brother knights. This fight with you was an impossible dream for you think you are an unbeatable foe and we stand no chance against you. But our king and his faithful and true son have gathered the armies of heaven and sent them to our aid in this great endeavor. What you first thought was going to be so easy to do in your murder of us, has suddenly been made much harder for you. We would have gladly let you take the life from us for the glory of our king. But now we have been made equal to you in strength, we can fight back to stop your sinister plan and save ourselves.

BOLD KNIGHT:

Once again I am in total agreement with my brothers in all things said. We are in the middle of two armies, large in size but differ in purpose. We side with our Eternal King, and his loyal son, The Lord Christ. We also stand firmly with our true brother angels in faith. Great is the danger we now face but greater is our courage and trust in our king El-Elyon (The Most High God.)

BOLD KNIGHT'S SECOND PRAYER:

Universal Sovereign Lord El-Shaddai (God Almighty), before your magnificent throne so high in the heavens I once again respectfully and humbly approach with my brother knights Brave Duke, Sir Romance A Lot, Richard the Deep Hearted and Prince Passion. Again we praise your glory and greatness.

Celestial Father, we thank you for sending your steadfast and true servants, the angels that now stand ready to engage in combat with this horrible Dark Soul. We all fight for your honor and great name. Father, we plead to you for strength and courage in this grand battle we are about to enter into. We pray for your great right hand, which is so mighty in war and has never been defeated. Many times it was you that helped your loyal servants of old in battles they fought in your name.

The Nation of Israel, particularly Joshua and David, that fought in your name. Because of your strength they were able to defeat their enemies. Your faithful servant and prophet Elijah, who would have surely been killed if he had failed on Mount Caramel against the false prophets of Baal. But your great hand rained down fire from heaven and proved to all that you were and still are the true God. It was truly you that caused the Baal prophets their doom. (1 Kings Chapter 18) It was your mighty power that saved King Hezekiah from the Assyrian army. 185,000 of their soldiers died in one night because of the power that you gave to your loyal angel. (2 Kings 19:20-35 and Isaiah 37:21-36)

Oh mighty Lord of Hosts, Jehovah of Armies. You are the

Supreme Universal Commander of a vast army of true angels, some of which are with us now. I pray in earnest to the warrior side of your great and magnificent mind. That part of you which is the undefeated warrior and will never lose at ANYTHING! May you instill that same fighting spirit inside of me and my brother knights and angels so that we give you the glory in this conflict. All praise to you, Sovereign Lord Yahweh God.

In the name of our Lord, the one who is Faithful and True, Jesus Christ, I pray this prayer for my brothers and me.

Amen

SUPREME UNIVERSAL COMMANDER, JEHOVAH GOD ASKS CHRIST:

"My son, what of the princess who has also said a prayer for divine guidance? What are your plans for her?" I have an idea on how to answer her prayer of help.

"Abba (Father), I will make her like the knights that love and serve her heart. I will give her the same powers, but different abilities that you gave them so that she can fight and help to defeat this mad Dark Soul."

"I am thinking the same, my son. Give unto her those powers."

BOLD EYE: As I am looking down upon the two armies, one good and one totally evil, separated by only about 20 yards apart, I again see the Holy Spirit come from the throne room of heaven. But this time, the light he represents is much brighter than those that empowered the knights. It glows very bright as it lands directly in the middle of the space between the Armies of Heaven and the dark forces of Hell. In an instant it disappears and now standing there is Queen Splendina.

But dressed as a princess she is no longer. She is now clothed in full battle gear like her servants the knights. On top of her head is a spiked, gold helmet that resembles something from the field of battle.

Her body was covered with a golden suit of light armor that shines like light from the throne of the true God. On the left side of her waist were three golden throwing knives. The right side of her waist held three knives as well. But something looked very unusual about all of them. Written across the armor on the upper part of her chest in the language of heaven, and translated into human understanding means "God's love conquers all evil."

Both of her arms are fitted in gold armor with raised writings and inscriptions even I do not understand and could not interpret. Encircled around the upper part of both her arms are gold bands. For some unknown reason to me, the band on her right arm is smaller in width than the one around her left arm.

On her feet are golden boots that come up to her knees, and each boot has a set of small wings on their heels. However, at the top of her right boot was an extra piece of armor that her left boot did not have. In her hands is a weapon like no other on the entire field of battle. It is a long golden pole with sharp blades on each end. I instantly recognize the blades as being made from the glowing majesty of God's throne.

THEN SHE SHOUTS . . .

My angelic brothers and my loyal knights. Our magnificent king and his glorious son have united us today to do battle against the dark and evil forces of Hell. To defeat this demented Dark Soul and send him back to his master as the total loser he is now and soon will be forever. (Revelation 20:7-10) Empowered we all are now to stop his lunacy and to show him that his hate will be overcome by the splendid power of love.

This day, we fight for the glory of our king and his son, The Christ. Let us not be faint in heart or faith, for we have truth and justice on our side. Dark Soul has mocked us and all of heaven with his cruel words and vile accusations. Today, we will right this unrightable wrong by soundly defeating this unbeatable foe and sending--------

DARK SOUL RUDELY INTERRUPTS QUEEN SPLENDINA: You bird brain moron Splendina! You think that because you've been given special powers by that fool king--------

QUEEN SPLENDINA CUTS DARK SOUL OFF WITH GREAT ANGER

IT'S TIME FOR YOU TO SHUT YOUR FOUL MOUTH AND FIGHT. LET'S FINISH THIS!!!!!

BOLD EYE: With those words, the wings on Queen Splendina's boots suddenly point up and she leaps high in the air toward Dark Soul, with her double-ended weapon spinning over her head. As she is about to land on the ground, Dark Soul draws his dark sword and blocks her blow. When she hits the ground, she crouches and spins her body and her weapon at the same time and jabs upward at his chin. Dark Soul, who has fought many a battle as well, instinctively jumps backward in time to miss her thrust by less than two inches.

With lightning speed, Queen Splendina stands halfway up and

twirls her weapon a little more than waist high, aiming for Dark Soul's midsection. Dark Soul was caught totally off guard by this move and he realized this too late, as her blade sliced across his upper chest. A yellowish-green liquid started to form where her blade cut him. (Yes humans, we spirit creatures do bleed and feel pain, believe it or not.)

Queen Splendina has just drawn first blood. The Battle for Brave Love was on.

BOLD KNIGHT SHOUTS: WE FOLLOW OUR QUEEN INTO BATTLE, FOR THE GLORY OF OUR KING AND HIS SON. LET'S FINISH THIS!!!!

BOLD EYE: Having shouted those words, God-inspired knights and angels alike both run and fly forward together, clashing into Dark Soul's demonic army. The loud sound of weapons crashing into each other is heard all over the battlefield, as knights, angels and demons meet in a titanic struggle for the sovereignty of God and the eternity of love. Ancient enemies that first started out as faithful brothers in heaven are now locked in deadly universal combat against each other.

Once again, old scores and personal grudges are being fought over for every time we angels have to do battle with our former brothers, they always remind us of past battles that were contested.

Two more conflicts of the past that involved Earth were the Battle of the Mid Ocean Ridge and the Ayers Rock Incident. The Mid Ocean Ridge War was waged when the demons wanted to raise this mountain range that encircles the Earth underwater in your oceans, to the surface. This would have caused mass flooding, destruction, and death on a global scale. The armies of

Heaven were sent to stop this mass catastrophe from happening and a fierce fight broke out. The Angels of the Invincible Spear and The Angels of the Celestial Light Swords were the main divine warriors who won this victory for heaven.

The Ayers Rock (aboriginal name Uluru) Incident occurred when certain demons were so fascinated by this natural Australian landmark, that they wanted to duplicate millions of copies all around the world. For some odd reason, most were to be placed in the whole of Europe. They even wanted to place hundreds in the very center of Rome, and also entirely surround the Colombian cities of Bogota' and Cali! Our magnificent King Eternal was against this stupid idea and once again a bitter fight broke out. The Dreadnaught Warriors and the Starlight Strikers fought to end this disastrous plan of theirs.

Across the huge battlefield of the great plain of Megiddo, (Revelation 16:16) I can see those grudges of old play out once again. My brother Archangels Fierce Blade, Courage Strike and the 12 War Blade Legions under their command, which include The Angels of the Invincible Spear and half of The Angels of the Infinite Arrow, who are heaven's best archers and their arrows always fly true, are battling very hard. Unknown to you humans, it was the arrows of these brave brothers that helped to defeat many of the enemies that the nation of Israel fought in the Old Testament of your bibles. They are now again fighting against Clydrok, the leader of the Varkinian Horde that they defeated at the Spectoxulus Quasar. Another ancient and bitter rivalry renewed.

But with Clydrok are the Tartummus hordes who also want bitter revenge for having been defeated by the 12 War Blade Legions at the American Revolution Battle of Saratoga, various battles of the French Revolution, and the Civil War Battle of Gettysburg.

This scenario is being played out all over the battlefield. As I gaze down more from heaven, I see the Supreme Seraphim Great Arm and the Stellar Star Sword Legions battling Molech, Chemosh, Zaltaxus, and Necotor, the Archduke of the Bratoxzumus Void with his filthy followers, the Chenarax. I see the Supreme Seraphim Thunder Hand leading the Dreadnaught Warriors against Wazlarx and his Dytharus Pit hordes. They last fought in your human World War II, in the battles for Europe.

I turn my head to the right and see the Supreme Seraphims Truth Sword, Brave Fire and the Starlight Strikers locked in a fierce struggle with the Evil Dratox, from the Latarzus Depths and his allies, the wicked Asmodai and his hellish 13 Hordes from the Necronomus Abysmal. Hand-to-hand they are fighting each other. Swords of light clashing mightily against swords and axes of darkness.

The knights are not left out of this spectacular battle. All of them are now engaged in combat with various demons too. Prince Passion and the ice demon Thorn, who is second in command of the northern regions of the Earth, are going at each other with great fury. Having the power from the Lord God equal to that of we spirit creatures, Prince Passion holds nothing back in his attack. But Thorn, who is known for his fighting abilities and for his love of the colder regions of the Earth, holds his own and refuses to give an inch.

Bold Knight's first opponent in this saga is the number three demon in charge from the southern region of the Earth, Slaytarq. A master swordsman, Bold Knight has fought many a foe winning most and losing some. But never have he and his brothers fought against adversaries as powerful as demons. Slaytarq is not known in the spirit realms as being a fighter, but rather a disrupter and a troublemaker. It is he and over 900,000 of his evil brothers that have caused much misery, pain, and suffering in South America alone.

As they meet in battle, Bold Knight took the offensive first by swinging his sword in a side strike. But Slaytarq easily blocks the blow. That is exactly what Bold Knight wanted him to do, for Bold Knight locks his sword with Slaytarq's and suddenly draws out a short sword from under his suit of armor and plunges it into the chest of Slaytarq. A loud scream of surprise and pain comes from his mouth as Bold Knight quickly withdrew his short sword and stepped back with a wry smile on his face.

The yellow-green liquid starts to flow out of his wound at a rapid pace. The demon is wounded in both body and pride, having been dealt such a serious blow so early in this great battle. He staggers backwards with a look of total disbelief and pain.

BOLD KNIGHT SPEAKS: Take that back to your evil master the devil, and tell him who did this to you. Tell him also that soon our Lord Christ will strike down both him and ALL who follow him in spirit and in flesh.

But Bold Knight has very little time to gloat because the demon Britaxorn 6 saw his evil brother bleeding, and rushes to his aid by engaging Bold Knight in a new fight. This raving mad lunatic demon is partially named after a part of the United Kingdom because 6 times in its history, he was the evil force behind the humans that wanted it destroyed.

The rest of the knights are locked in deadly combat against the dark forces of Hell too. About five yards away from Prince Passion, Sir Romance A Lot's opponent is Psytarso, a very foul demon that helped to start and later carry out the Nanjing, Rwanda, Tiananmen Square, and Srebrenica massacres. Brave

Duke is entangled in a serious fight with Murdermokk, a particularly nasty foe that is known in the spirit realms as "The Assassin of Hell." It is this psychopathic demon that is responsible for some of your human history's most famous assassinations. And the list is not short.

In no particular order of importance or dates, some of them are as follows: Dr. Martin Luther King Jr., Abraham Lincoln, Mahatma Gandhi, Benazir Bhutto, John Lennon, John and Robert Kennedy, Julius Caesar, Yitzhak Rabin, Indira Gandhi and later her son Rajiu Gandhi, Alexander Litvinenko, Anna Politkovskaya, Empress Myeongseong (Queen Min of Korea), King Henry IV, and one of the most history-changing assassinations in your human existence, Arch Duke Franz Ferdinand. It was this one that helped to start your World War I which later helped to influence the absolute, totally crazed tyrant Adolf Hitler to start World War II.

Not to be left out, Richard the Deep Hearted is trading blows with Jeerzius, the number four demon that left heaven. This adversary is no stranger to humanity, especially all who live and have lived in the countries of the USA, Mexico, and Canada. These are the nations in which he and his vile followers choose to work their evil deeds in.

Not side-by-side, but very close to each other, I see the knights in a furious battle against Hell. This is their style, to always fight close to each other. Just in case one falls, the others are there to come to his aid. I have witnessed this many, many times throughout their history and am much impressed by it. Their battle with the frightful dragon Terrorwolx was one example in which all of them had to fight together to defeat it. Also, it was in this battle that Bold Knight and Richard the Deep Hearted suffered serious leg injuries from the spiked tail of Terrorwolx.

We angels do the same when we have to go against our former brothers and now sworn enemies. Your human Spanish Civil War was one particular war in which we were packed so close to each other in battle, which we later joked about it after the war was over.

As Bold Knight is in a difficult struggle with the demon Britaxorn 6, he takes time to quickly glance around at his brothers to see how they are doing. As the knight leader, he takes responsibility for the well-being of his fellow knights. Satisfied that they are more than holding their own, he shouts a new concern.

"MY BROTHERS, WE MUST BE WATCHFUL OF OUR QUEEN. MAKE SURE NO HARM COMES TO HER."

But Queen Splendina is doing quite well for herself.

Having sliced Dark Soul across his chest and opening up a good-sized wound, Splendina now presses her attack. With her dual-bladed weapon spinning in her hands, she set upon him with even more fury. Dark Soul had no time to recover from his injury as he is now forced to defend himself even more from her rage. The cruel attack he earlier gave her and her knights in words, he was now getting back in a ferocious assault.

His sword met her weapon many times as she unleashes blow after blow. But remember, this is the number two demon in all of Hell. And having been around for countless ages, he too learned a trick or two about fighting. Though he was mainly blocking, he also was managing to attack her as well. Dark Soul decides he would now use one of those tricks he learned throughout the centuries. The technique he decides to use requires her to strike at him with an overhead blow. While waiting for her to give him the opportunity he wanted, he first has to keep her at bay. This was proving harder to do because of the dual threat nature of her weapon. She can attack him more ways and much faster than a regular sword.

Splendina's attack is coming at him from all directions. Rapid, near-fatal slashes to his midsection. Savage thrusts from all directions to his head. Life threatening, spinning death blows to his head and neck. Her assault is relentless. Then she gives him the opening he was looking for. After a vicious thrust to his neck misses because he barely moves out of the way in time, she then swings her weapon in an overhead arc in a vicious blow designed to split Dark Soul's skull in half. With the skills of a centuries upon centuries old foe, Dark Soul very fast does a half turn with his body and as he turns, his dark sword turns with him in a downward swing.

Because of the fact that Splendina's weapon is lighter and faster than Dark Soul's sword, hers is the first to complete its path to find empty space. That is what saves her from critical injury, for his sword was on its way to deal her a serious blow. Had her weapon connected in some way with Dark Soul, she would have stood still long enough for his sword to connect with her body full force.

His sword, completing its down swing, was now coming from an upward angle at her. Splendina realized too late what Dark Soul is about to do and the blow he is about to strike. She reacts to this danger by jumping a good ten feet in the air and at the same time turning a backward somersault. But it was not soon enough, as the left side of his sword slices into the right side of her right leg where there is bare skin and no armor. As she lands, her right leg buckles and she almost falls sideways, but she quickly finds her balance again. The two combatants are now about eight feet apart, glaring at each other through slotted eyes, stored up with eons of hatred.

DARK SOUL SNEERS: Well, I guess that little cut makes this fight a little more even.

QUEEN SPLENDINA: We will NEVER be even, you foul fool. You, your evil master, all your wicked brothers and all the humans throughout time under your control have sown so much despair, destruction, and death. The ONLY way we will ever be even is when our king's son destroys you and your unholy, corrupted allies once and for all. (Again, Revelation 20:7-10) As for now, one of us is going back to Hell today, AND I DON'T THINK IT'S ME!

Having said those words, Splendina lifts her two-headed spear in one hand and twirls it over her head very fast as she starts to run at Dark Soul. Before she can even reach him to strike her next blow, Dark Soul leaps high in the air and turns an upside-down half twist. This is so that he could swing his dark sword at her head and at an angle she least expected a strike to come from. And it almost found its mark had she not crouched down very low, as the blow barely misses her by less than an inch.

The instant Dark Soul's feet hit the ground, he is under another all-out attack, for Splendina is on him again with even more fury. Back and forth the two combatants battle, swinging angry blows, then playing defense and blocking. They spar and parry, death strike after death strike, the two eternal adversaries are heaving at each other. Attacking, and then defending. Offense, then defense. Neither one giving an inch. Dark Soul's motivation is his hatred for all that is good and his enmity for heaven. Queen Splendina fights for love, its creator, and the deepness of love that every woman has in her heart, and wants to give and receive unselfishly.

MEANWHILE, IN THE MAGNIFICENT THRONE ROOM OF HEAVEN, THE KING OF KINGS AND LORD OF LORDS JESUS CHRIST, AND HIS MAJESTIC FATHER, THE UNIVERSAL SOVEREIGN LORD YAHWEH GOD ARE GAZING DOWN UPON THIS GRAND BATTLE BEING FOUGHT.

CHRIST: Abba, your decision to make the knights equal in power to their demonic foes was a very wise one. Their leader Bold Knight has inflicted a serious blow to Slaytarq already. And his brother knights are fending for themselves quite well too. Also, Queen Splendina is defending our glory and her honor against Dark Soul. But we know that Dark Soul is full of tricks and she has been wounded by one of them. We also know that soon he will use more of them against her.

Why let this battle be fought now when your day of wrath is so very close? I will soon righteously give both humans and demons their reward or punishment.

ELOHIM GOD: You, your faithful brothers and humanity have been fighting against Hell and its wicked rulers since the first rebellion began. The sovereignty of Heaven's throne and who's right to rule it are in question here. This is just one more battle in a war that has spanned millennium upon millennium.

As you have stated before, soon *you* will execute my righteous judgment against the earth and its visible and invisible rulers. (Revelation 19:11-21) For now, I will permit this war to occur and for it to answer the human question of whether or not love truly conquers hate in ALL its reprehensible forms.

My son, instruct Michael to take command of this war. He is now The General in charge of strategy.

BOLD EYE: Courage Strike and Fierce Blade along with the 12 War Blade Legions are meshed in an intense struggle with Clydrok and his Varkinian Hordes and the Tartummus armies of Hell. The anger of ages was once again on display as these two eternal enemies fight each other again in a deadly duel of universal supremacy. The Angels of the Invincible Spear, Angels of the Furious Swords, and The Angels of the Celestial Light Swords are fighting their former brothers with the same, if not more intensity that is being returned against them. But for a reason unknown to me, half of the Angels of the Infinite Arrow and the Angels of the Invincible Spear are not here on the battlefield.

I have seen them both in close combat and separately in the firing of their divinely guided arrows. It was one of these Infinite Arrows that struck down your human King Herod for his arrogance and his thoughtless stupidity toward God. (Acts 12:6-23)

While Courage Strike is commanding the 12 War Blade Legions, his brother Archangel Fierce Blade is engaged in a knock-down, all-out fight with Clydrok. Sword of light meets once again, with an axe of darkness. But to Clydrok, this battle is much more personal because of the humiliating defeat he suffered at the Spectoxulus Quasar battle. He wants revenge in the worst way and his fighting shows it as he lets loose his hatred upon the Supreme Seraphim, holding nothing back. Powerful swinging skull-crushing overhand blows, axe tip thrusts to any part of the angel's body were coming at an incessant rate. But this is one of the most powerful angels in all of Heaven and he proves his fighting prowess as he retaliates with the same fury. Clydrok often has to play defense as well because of the angel's well-timed blows to all parts of his body, too.

Heaven versus Hell

The Supreme Seraphim Great Arm, leader of the Stellar Star Sword Angels, is still locked in a deadly, uneven match against Molech and Chemosh, the rulers of the Northern and Southern regions of the earth. They have sought him out specifically on the battlefield, before this skirmish began. Their sick reasoning for doing this is, now is their chance to do battle and maybe even wound a Supreme Seraphim. Should they accomplish this fiendish task, this would give them "bragging rights" in the nether realms. Now high above the great plain of Megiddo where many other personal battles are already being fought, so too was this one. One Supreme Seraphim versus two very strong demons.

On the ground, Great Arm's angelic brothers The Angels of the Stellar Star Swords are in an immortal contest with Zaltaxus, the demon ruler of the Eastern regions of the earth. Joining with Zaltaxus once again and leading his hellish army in this conflict is Necotor, the Archduke of the Bratoxzumus Void and his most filthy and demented followers, the Chenarax.

I mention that they are together again because they love to pair up and inflict so much pain and misery upon you humans. As of this moment, they have teamed up to extend for as long as possible, your human wars in Syria and Afghanistan. And various conflicts in Africa, The Middle East, and Ukraine.

Back and forth these ageless rivals fight. Swords of starlight versus dark swords, axes, and trazokk's of darkness. (A trazokk is a short spear in which half of it is a handle, and the other half is a long spiral blade instead of a flat-tipped blade at its end. A very deadly weapon of evil.) Former friends now irreversible enemies.

I gaze upon them as they fight each other, and my heart once more feels remorse. I think back again on the good times we had before the rebellion in heaven. The eons it took us to help our king construct the 77 galaxies of the Zardayius Realms. Our Grand Creator was so generous to us angels that he actually let us design 12 of the solar systems! How thoughtful and wonderful he truly is.

Looking down upon the battlefield again, I see the fourth Supreme Seraphim Thunder Hand entwined in a lethal scuffle with Wazlarx, the leader of the Dytharus Pit hordes. Thunder Hand's weapon of choice is named the Sword of Valiant Thunder. It takes after part of his name, because his sword has the power to launch thunder strikes, lightning bolts, or anything else that our kings command.

You humans have proof of the power of his mighty sword in your bibles once again, for it was him who destroyed the immoral cities of Sodom and Gomorrah by raining sulfur down on them. (Genesis 19)

Its special powers are only put to use when he is told to use them. But in this battle, he is a loyal angel fighting toe-to-toe against a disloyal demon. Sword of Heaven battling a trizokk from Hell. (A trizokk is a three-pronged, trident weapon in which the blades resemble those of a trazokk, instead of pointed spikes. Another very dangerous evil weapon)

Bold Knight is still in a death duel with the demon Britaxorn 6, as well the other knights too. Each of them are locked in cosmic combat versus malevolent forces as the battle for Brave Love rages on. In a small circle of the large, decisive battlefield of Megiddo, an unusual contest is taking place. Humans super-empowered by the very hand of the Supreme Universal Commander Jehovah God going against the dark, demonic forces of Hell.

Britaxorn 6 is starting to become very overconfident against the knight leader. Having withstood a fierce assault from the knight, he is feeling secure in the fact that he can overcome him and make heaven look foolish for granting the knights extraordinary powers. So he decides to press his attack against Bold Knight more. The demon is cutting, jabbing, and slicing from all sides. Upward sword thrusts. Aggressive, death dealing spinning attack combinations. Mighty overhead deathblows that the knight has to use his glowing shield to block because of the sheer power of the blows. It is this arrogant attitude that is his undoing. A downfall that has been centuries upon centuries overdue.

Britaxorn 6 swings a powerful overhead strike designed to either kill the knight or unnerve him so much that he can quickly launch another strike at a more vital part of his body before he can recover from the first disruptive blow. What the demon did not plan for was Bold Knight blocking this crushing blow with the outer right edge of his shield. Bold Knight, on purpose, tilted his shield this way because this is an old defensive trick he learned through many a battle. Its purpose is to lull an opponent into thinking that the entire shield actually stopped the blow.

What this defensive maneuver really does is to potentially expose an adversary to an unprotected and unexpected blow from behind his shield. As the blow lands on the shield edge, Bold Knight could see the whole left side of the demon's body unprotected and vulnerable. The eternal knight swung his sword in a right-sided, cross body arc and sliced the demon from the left side of its body to the right.

A scream of pure pain and fear came from the demon's wicked

mouth and he tried to retreat by flying away backwards. Bold Knight sees this and he once again drew his short sword from the hilt of his long sword. But this time instead of plunging it into his foe like he did earlier with Slaytarq, he hurls it like a guided spear at the demon. It did not miss its mark as it penetrates the middle of the demon's chest, and causing the greenish-yellow liquid to flow from a second wound.

Britaxorn 6 dropped from the sky when the short sword hit him. Screaming in even more pain, he hit the ground hard and rolled onto his back. He was just in time to see Bold Knight moving towards him with his sword held high, ready to deliver the final blow.

From less than five yards away, Dark Soul was in the fight of his life with a heavenly inspired Splendina. Because of her furious, determined attack after attack, he truly had his hands very full. But when he heard Britaxorn 6's screams of pain and saw what Bold Knight was about to do, he had to act very fast to save him. Dark Soul somehow managed to disengage himself from Splendina by just running over to the fallen demon. But at the same time, he has to keep a watchful eye on Splendina and her very dangerous assault.

Dark Soul reached his fallen comrade just a half-second before Bold Knight was close enough to deliver the final blow to Britaxorn 6. Spinning his sword over his head, he steps in front of his fallen evil soldier and proceeds to launch a counter strike against Bold Knight. This attack slowed down the knight leader and surprised him too, for he did not expect the demon leader would arrive so fast to help. Queen Splendina was closing in very fast on Dark Soul's right side. With her uncanny, yet deadly dual bladed weapon, she too twirls it over her head and then let loose a blow aimed squarely at the demon's head. Dark Soul deflects her blow and throws a quick blow or two of his own to back her up some. By this time, Bold Knight is once again on the offensive against the demon. It is now a two-on-one battle, as Queen Splendina and the gallant Bold Knight are locked in a celestial grudge match of infinite proportions against their demonic adversary of the ages.

Back and forth the three combatants intensely struggle. Once again, attacking then defending. Defending, and then attacking. Queen Splendina and her divine double-bladed spear, and Bold Knight's sword of Truth and Light, battling the vilest Dark Soul and his twisted "Sword of Darkness and Hate."

Dark Soul knows he cannot not keep the two God-inspired combatants at bay much longer. He can barely repel Queen Splendina's ferocious assault against him and to now have not only her, but her knight leader also to contend with, was more than he can handle right now. So taking after his evil master, he knows he has to once again dig into his bag of tricks.

After fending off one particular series of attacks by the deadly duo, he just turns and runs, expecting them to give chase, which is exactly what happens. Suddenly Dark Soul pulls a small dagger from the handle of his sword and quickly spins around to face the two. But even before he was fully turned, the dagger was flying on its way towards Splendina, blade first.

Splendina had mere eye-blink milliseconds to react. But now being a superior warrior queen, she is much faster than the short knife speeding towards her. She easily does a half turn with her body and watches in annoyance as it sails past her. Though it misses its mark with her, it found another target in the upper middle back of the ice demon Thorn, who was still fighting Prince Passion.

The cold demon screams in total shock and pain as the dagger lodges in him. Then he makes a big mistake by letting his guard down to reach around and try to pull the knife out. Prince Passion saw this and instantly realizes he needs to attack. So he swings his sword in a straight line across his body. The tip of his sword slices into Thorn's body from right to left. The cut is deep enough for the greenish-yellow liquid to start flowing out very fast.

Thorn knew he was finished fighting in this contest for he has sustained two very serious wounds. The demon takes a very wild look at Prince Passion and simply flies off in utter humiliation and stunned defeat.

Dark Soul is in complete shock as The Law of Unintended Consequences has just caught up with him. For centuries upon centuries, he has used this unpredictable law against humanity as a whole. And it has served his evil purposes very well. More recently, he and his unholy master the Devil; have used this law to their atrocious advantage in the aftermath of the second United States invasion of Iraq.

Now having unintentionally helped his bitter rivals the knights and Queen Splendina defeat one of his most powerful Earth demons, a look of stark fear spreads across his face as he realizes he is in even more trouble, and he is about to fight even harder.

MEANWHILE IN HEAVEN, THE MIGHTY ARCHANGEL MICHAEL IS GIVING INSTRUCTIONS.

Michael summons the remaining Angels of the Invincible Spear to him. He instructs them to divide their forces in half and launch a dual attack on the rear left flank and rear right flank of Dark

Soul's totally demonic army. Because of the fact that Queen Splendina and her knights are engaging Dark Soul in eternal universal combat, Dark Soul cannot give directions to his unholy allies as their General. This proves to be a very costly mistake in his treachery against Heaven. Another one of many he has made throughout the millenniums.

Without hesitation, these loyal brothers fly down to the battle and begin their twin assaults on the swarms of Hell. Michael then calls the remaining Angels of the Infinite Arrow to him. He instructs them to unleash their Arrows of Truth upon Dark Soul's hordes. Instantly, thousands of my brothers fly down to the battlefield and take up positions around the great plain of Megiddo. They pull out their golden bows with silver arrows and proceed to rain down wave after wave of divinely guided arrows that never fail to hit their intended target, upon the demonic hordes of Dark Soul. Screams of pain came from the many demons that are being struck by these holy arrows.

Wazlarx is the first demon leader to see the storm of heavenly arrows that are raining down on his gruesome followers. He quickly orders a massive counteroffensive by his own dark archers who are on standby, waiting to be called up from the Dytharus Pit of Hell. They quickly join their depraved leader and start to launch their own dark arrows in return. Joining them in this are the demon archers of Dratox and Necotor for they too call up their vile forces from Hell to help in this aerial battle of arrows. Intently watching this intense, white-hot warfare, I see loyal heavenly angels, God-empowered knights, and a Christ-backed battle queen waging a righteous war against sinister demons from Hell and their corrupt allies of the Earth. With arrows flying all over the field and personal grudges being fought over in hand-to-hand clashes, this has truly become a war of monumental intensity on both sides.

Dark Soul is in very big trouble now. He started all this by opening his big, cruel mouth and criticizing, demeaning and degrading the emotion of love, King Eternal and his wonderful son The Christ, The Century Princess, and then her knights. Now he is facing Queen Splendina, Bold Knight, and Prince Passion all by himself. The godly energized queen alone is more than enough for him to deal with. Then he had to fight her and Bold Knight. Now as the three combatants raise their weapons once again and start towards him, he knows he has to do something to equalize the odds very fast.

Very fast are the key words here because Dark Soul's situation is about to get even worse still.

Having dispatched the first demonic foes they encountered and other antagonists too, (Sir Romance a Lot defeated Psytarso with a strike that nearly severed the demon's arm off. Then he made short work of Hardajon and Iqarzuk 4, before having a long fight with Razklavor before vanquishing him. Brave Duke outlasted Murdermokk with a blow to the chest followed by a quick, spinning slash to the back. Baxwarnth, Plazquar, and Obaflarn followed. Richard the Deep Hearted overcame Jeerzius by doing the same tilted shield move that Bold Knight used to defeat Britaxorn 6 and sliced him across the eyes. He then beat Hurlorwn, Dartorlius, Rastulor, and Rocctorwal.) The three knights looked for their queen, only to find her, their leader Bold Knight, and Prince Passion advancing towards Dark Soul with swords in fighting position. Not wanting to be left out of the master demon's possible demise, they too join in this soon-to-be showdown.

Dark Soul's luck has now changed from bad to worse to much, much worse. He is now facing Queen Splendina and her five Knights of Brave Love all by himself. Seeing that the tables ·

have turned against him, he knows he has to get help to himself immediately. Dark Soul raises his sword above his head, points it skyward and quickly mumbles something under his breath.

It is Zaltaxus, Molech, and Chemosh who first feel the dire summons of help from their fiendish leader. Engaged in bouts with Supreme Seraphim's and Archangels, each of them just simply stops fighting and flies away. So too does Wazlarx, Dratox, and Asmodai when they too feel Dark Soul's urgent call for assistance. All the supreme seraphim's and archangels were about to give chase, but each are thwarted by new demonic attackers coming at them to take up where their leaders left off in the fighting. Asmodai is the only one who thinks to bring with him some of his inhuman followers.

The knights and Queen Splendina are closing in on Dark Soul. With steely-eyed determination and divine anger on their faces, they surrounded him, weapons at the ready. Then Bold Knight yells with fury.

BOLD KNIGHT: You mad dog Dark Soul! You caused all this because of your arrogance, hate, and pride. But today, those too will be buried with you and your cowardly hordes. In the name of our magnificent king and his righteous son, we now finish this battle.

DARK SOUL: (WITH A WICKED SMILE ON HIS FACE) Not so fast, you idiots. Just like I have to go through the forces of Heaven to finish off you stupid knights and your boar queen, you now have to go through the forces of Hell even more, to finish me off. You might want to glance up and around you now. Eyes turn upwards just in time to see the demonic leaders of Earth and Hell swiftly flying in to help Dark Soul. The knights broke their circle around Dark Soul and spread themselves about two feet apart, backs to each other in another circle around their queen. They then raise their swords and shields in defensive fighting formation.

The flying demon rulers are about 100 feet away from their leader and the knights when the wings on Queen Splendina's boots point skyward and she leaps high in the air. As she rises higher, she switches her weapon from her left hand to her right hand, then spins backwards to her right and flings her left arm out with great force. The unknown writing on the armor of her arm I did not recognize earlier when I first seen the newly transformed Splendina, suddenly flies off the armor and become lethal missiles aimed at the demon leaders who are now less than twenty feet away.

Had Splendina waited maybe a second longer before launching her surprise attack, she would have pierced all the first wave of the demon leaders with her projectiles. But the mistiming of her unexpected attack gave most of them enough time to evade the missiles coming at them. Dratox was not so fortunate and neither are eight of Asmodai's followers, as the missiles find their marks in various parts of their bodies.

Screams of agony once again filled the air as they instantly fall from the sky and hit the ground very hard. Again Splendina changes her weapon, this time from her right hand to her left hand, spins backwards to her left and this time throws her right arm out, aiming at Asmodai's second wave of attackers. The unknown characters on the armor of her right arm once again flew off, sailing towards the demons. They too meet the same fate as their profane brothers as they fall from the sky in pain and disbelief as the divine darts hit them.

A small third wave of Asmodai's hideous hordes was still

coming at Splendina and are closing fast. But she has an answer for them. Sheathing her twin bladed weapon behind her back, she takes out the three small throwing knives from her waist in each hand and fires them at her would be attackers. As the knives fly to their targets, they suddenly separate into three more duplicate pieces. So instead of six, there are now 24. Once again, cries of pain fills the air as the blades hit their satanic targets, dropping then from the sky. The demon Wardyvis is blinded when two of them hit him in both eyes.

By this time, the demon rulers have landed and now are engaged in deadly combat with the knights. Bold Knight is locked in a fierce bout with Zaltaxus and so too are Prince Passion and Richard the Deep Hearted with Molech and Chemosh respectively. Brave Duke's duel with Wazlarx is heating up with frantic intensity very fast and so too is Sir Romance a Lot opposing Asmodai.

It is a well-known fact in Heaven and on Earth (to those of you humans who believe) that demons are masters of trickery and deception. (Genesis 3:1-15, 2 Corinthians 4:4, Revelation 12:7-12,17) And in this war, that fact is no exception. The demon Asmodai divided the followers he bought with him into two parts. One part will attack with him from the air, while the second will confront the knights from the ground. Their aerial assault failed greatly because of Queen Splendina's unforeseen attacks. From her position in the air, she can see a medium group of about fifty demons coming straight for the knights. Splendina drops back to the ground and twists the handle of her dual-bladed spear. The blades released from the main shaft, but they are now suspended on each end by a five-foot shiny golden chain. The battle queen ran towards the oncoming dark soldiers of Asmodai with her newly changed weapon twirling over her head.

Splendina met the horde head on, with another all-out, vicious and furious assault. With her double-edged chained weapon spinning and attacking Asmodai's followers from all positions, they can do nothing to launch any kind of offense against her. The unpredictable nature of her weapon spinning so fast and from so many angles made the chance of any successful counterattack by the demons very risky at best, and possibly causing serious injury at worst. In this case, to stay well clear of her deadly, dual-bladed chained destroyer was presently the best option.

Dark Soul has stepped back from all the fighting his troublesome generals are engaged in with the knights and is now watching each match with great interest. Now finally having slowed down, he can feel the pulsing pain from the cut Splendina gave him earlier. The vital "Splood" (SPirit bLOOD) was now covering most of his chest and he suddenly feels very weak. But he regains himself and glances around him. All over the battlefield, he could see fallen demons in various stages of suffering. Their moans of anguish are filling his ears and making him feel some sort of pity for them. Normally when he and his diabolical followers inflict misery in so many ways upon humanity, he revels in cruel delight and feels no remorse. But now that it's his own wicked minions, he feels a little . . . just a little grief.

Not to be left out, there are angels with wounds as well. He notices too that there were many more demons lying on the field than angels. And there are also other smaller contests being fought in the air and on the ground.

The Supreme Seraphim Great Arm and his Angels of the Stellar Star Swords have finally managed to defeat the abhorrent companions of Molech, Chemosh, and Zaltaxus after a bitter test. But Necotor and his ghoulish fiends from the Bratoxzumus Void, the Chenarax, are more of a challenge. It takes special help from The Angels of the Invincible Spear to vanquish these dark adversaries.

Now free from this engagement of war, the Supreme Seraphim Great Arm and the legions of angels under his present command, the Stellar Star Sword Angels and The Angels of the Invincible Spear, join the Supreme Seraphim Thunder Hand and the Dreadnaught Warriors to finish their strife with Wazlarx's Dytharus Pit hordes. With the Angels of the Infinite Arrow helping with their divinely guided arrows, they soon overcome the archers of Hell that are firing back in retaliation at them. Then the rest of this hellish army was sent back to where they came from, having been soundly defeated.

The two Supreme Seraphim now divide their two armies and sent them to finish the other conflicts that still remained. Great Arm and The Angels of the Stellar Star Swords went to help the Archangels Fierce Blade, Courage Strike, the Angels of the Furious Swords and the 12 War Blade Legions do fervent battle against Clydrok and his Varkinian hordes and the Tartummus Hordes from the Satazorous Foul Cave.

Thunder Hand and his Dreadnaught Warriors went to assist his fellow Supreme Seraphims Truth Sword, Brave Fire, and the Starlight Strikers to conquer Dratox and Asmodai's 13 Hordes from the Necronomus Abysmal.

With their master Asmodai away battling the knights, these demons are putting up a very hard fight, so to make him proud of their efforts. Asmodai is known to punish his hordes if he feels they did not fight hard enough or if they did not cause extreme suffering to humans or the Earth. It is because of this sick logic that humanity and now angels are having more of a difficult struggle than normal.

The knights are still in ferocious matches of epic intensity against the sinister rulers of Hell and the Earth. I say epic intensity because never in all the millenniums since the rebellion of heaven have I seen such hard-hitting, unrestrained fighting. They are in the very faces of their unholy antagonists mounting their potent assaults, not giving an inch. All the centuries of agony these cruel, malicious creatures have inflicted upon mankind as a whole, they are now receiving back in the form of a relentless retaliation from the God blessed knights.

Bold Knight is very much engaged in an eternal death match with Zaltaxus. After one such fierce exchange of sword versus trazokk, the demon steps back from the contest and glares with much malice at the courageous knight. Then like his evil master Dark Soul, he speaks with much arrogance in his voice.

ZALTAXUS: I guess this is your revenge for my directing the abominable dragon Terrorwolx to slay you mud-for-brains knights. It was under my influence and control then and it almost succeeded in yours and Richard the Chicken Hearted's demise. You can thank me for all the scars you now have.

BOLD KNIGHT, FURIOUS WITH ANGER REPLIES: You dare to mock my brother's name after confessing that you used that filthy beast to almost kill us? I am going to send you back to your evil master in pieces!!!!!

With that, Bold Knight launches into a raging offensive against Zaltaxus. Sword thrusts to every area of the demon's body. Massive swinging blows to his head. The knight even used his golden shield to not only block against his trazokk counterattack, but to assail as well. It was a hammer-like blow from Bold Knight which the demon blocks that shatters the spiral blade part of his trazokk that bought Dark Soul back to the reality of the situation. He needs to help another of his evil cohorts or else.

Picking up a trazokk and a trizokk from the battlefield, he sprints over to where Zaltaxus is trying his best to defend himself from the knight's powerful attack. With his right hand, Dark Soul once again spars with the knight leader with the trazokk he exchanged his dark sword for. While doing this, he tossed the trizokk to Zaltaxus. The two wicked companions then began a coordinated assault against the knight leader.

Splendina and her newly transformed weapon are holding off a much larger crowd of demons than she first encountered. Spinning and twirling herself and her even-more dangerous dual-chained weapon, she can now attack from a distance. This is an advantage that she exploits to her benefit. She presses her offensive against the hordes of Hell so much that they are forced to retreat. There is no way that any of them can move inside the range of her weapon to strike her.

Seeing that she holds the upper hand by forcing them to back off, she stops her deadly attack and starts running back to where Dark Soul is entwined in battle with Bold Knight. With revenge on her mind, she is more than determined to be done with him once and for all.

Dark Soul was now in a position to see her charging at him, with a look of total fury and rage on her face. Even more fearful to him is her devastating, gyrating weapon which he instantly knew he is no match for. Not wanting to confront her in any way or form, he broke off his part of the assault against Bold Knight and flew off to better assess the present situation.

As soon as he was high enough to see most of the battlefield, he knew he was losing badly. All over the field, most of his dark army were either wounded or had retreated. The only battles still being fought are very close to their conclusion, as four of the Seven Supreme Seraphim along with the angels under their command are in the last stages of decimating Dark Soul's hideous hordes.

The full realization of his failed attempt to defame heaven, kill the knights, and then to crush the deep love that all women have in their hearts makes Dark Soul even more mad and vengeful. So angry in fact that he decides he will redeem himself before returning to his sinful master. The human expression "when hell breaks loose" looks like the perfect time to happen now.

Queen Splendina starts to chase after Dark Soul when he evaded her by flying off. But something in her now super-charged instincts tells her to look after her knights before she leaps. She takes a quick glance at them to see that they are still locked in gripping confrontations with the demon rulers. But out of the corner of her left eye, she sees the demon hordes that she had on the run before, have regrouped and divided into two clusters, one larger than the other. Both are closing in on the ground and in the air, to swarm her God-blessed, intrepid knights once again.

Splendina has to make a split second decision. Either she chase after Dark Soul to take her revenge for all the suffering he has caused to humanity and for this war he started, or to stay and help her loyal knights who have served her heart faithfully through the unfailing passing of time.

She chooses to stay and help her loyal companions. And to unleash another fearful weapon in her lethal arsenal.

Splendina quickly twists the handle of her chained, dual-bladed destroyer and the chains on each end disappear back into its handle. Sheathing her weapon behind her back, she unclasped first the smaller gold band around her upper right arm, and then closed it to where it was a circle again. She then tosses it up in the air ahead of the smaller crowd of demons. She does the same to the larger width band around her upper left arm, tossing it the air, ahead of the larger band of the advancing demons.

Each band starts to rapidly spin round and round, faster and faster. The faster they spin, the more the air around them picks up speed and force. In front of both advancing hordes of demons, there are now two small cyclones in motion.

Splendina then unhooks the extra piece of armor from her right leg and aims it at the demons that are about to overrun her knights. Immediately the winds being created in the midst of the hordes by the spinning bands, changes direction and now are being guided by the piece of armor Splendina was holding. All three pieces now form a guided cyclonic weapon, aimed at the hordes of Hell. Wherever she directs the piece of armor, the winds now follow, fiercely blowing away and scattering whatever is in front of her.

So much wind velocity is being created by the rapidly spinning bands and armor, that the demon hordes that are about to close in on the knights cannot not keep their footing or their balanced flight, and try to fly away from the now uncanny whirlwind weapon that the three pieces has formed. The force of the guided winds are now dispersing demons in every direction, thus ending their would-be swarming attack against the knights.

Having dominion over almost all of Hell and the Earth demons, and also having nothing to lose anymore, Dark Soul's deranged plan is to now call into the fray ALL of Hell and ALL of the Earth demons that did not first join the battle. Very quickly, more and more hordes start to appear in the air and on the ground. Dark Soul smiles in evil glee. Maybe . . . just maybe, his evil master will be proud of the turmoil and the totally reckless chaos he caused on this day.

IN THE MAJESTIC PALACE OF HEAVEN, THE ARCHANGEL MICHAEL SPEAKS:

I see what this mad fool Dark Soul is presently doing. He is unleashing all of Hell into this war. We must not let this insane plan of his succeed. Let us ALL go and totally finish this hostility for now.

Having said those words, Michael takes up his mighty golden sword and flies from heaven to the great plain of Megiddo. Behind him are millions upon millions upon millions of the armies of heaven in full battle gear, ready to join their brothers to end this feud. When Dark Soul looks up and see the myriads of angels led by the archangel Michael, he knew this part of his rebellion was over.

He knows he cannot compete and win anymore. For some odd reason, his defeat at The Battle of the Grand Canyon flashed in his mind for a moment. (This contest happened when Dark Soul joined with the ice demon Thorn and his icy hordes to first move, then divide this great American landmark between the northern European countries of Finland, Norway, Sweden, Denmark and Iceland for their own sick reasons. Michael and the 12 War Blade Legions took up the cause of heaven and put a stop to this totally insane plan.)

Remembering how Michael almost killed him then, he decides it is time to leave. Better to retreat like a scared dog than to fight on and become a dead lion. Besides, he still has a little time left to torment humanity more before Earth's (and his) day of judgment. (Again, Revelation 19:11-21)

With malice on their dark faces and total contempt for heaven in their hearts, all of Dark Soul's hordes either disengaged from their ongoing fights or picked themselves up off the field of battle and retreated to where they came from before this war started.

The Battle for Brave Love was over.

For now . . . .

Queen Splendina and her knights looked around them as their demonic foes all withdrew with light speed. At first, they did not know why this was happening, as the look on their faces shows total confusion. But when the battlefield and the skies all around them became filled with many more millions and millions of angels in full battle gear, they quickly understood why Dark Soul and his evil-minded hordes had withdrawn so fast. He did not want to have any more confrontations with heaven for now and especially did not want to clash again with the mighty archangel Michael, who is leading this final charge.

The air and the field of battle is now filled with warrior angels of every shape and size wearing "I am fully ready to do battle against anything that comes my way" looks on their faces and in their hearts. However, the expression on the knights' faces changes from confusion to awe when they see this majestic, heavenly army all around them. For a moment, being in the presence of so many angels overwhelms their senses to the po-

Bold Knight versus Dark Soul

int where they cannot move a muscle. It is Bold Knight who first regains his senses, drops his sword and shield, then goes down to both knees and bows his head in respect. The rest of the knights and their queen follow his lead and did the same.

QUEEN SPLENDINA: My true angelic brothers, we bow in reverence not to you, (Colossians 2:18, Revelation 19:10, Revelation 22:8,9) but to our King Eternal and his son, the Prince of Peace Christ for this great honor they have bestowed upon us lowly humans. For them to have sent you to help us to defeat Dark Soul and his cursed hordes, we are eternally grateful for. We thank them and we thank you for your loyalty and service to our king and his son. We give all praise and glory to him who is seated on the magnificent throne of heaven, and our Lord Christ, who is patiently standing at his right hand. (Romans 8:34, Ephesians 1:20, Colossians 3:1)

While she is talking, the mighty Archangel Michael and the four Supreme Seraphim's who led this battle, Truth Sword, Brave Fire, Thunder Hand, and Great Arm fly over to where Queen Splendina and her knights are. They hover in the air, side-by-side just above them. Then Thunder Hand speaks.

THUNDER HAND: Rise to your feet, my earthly sister and brothers.

ACTION: Queen Splendina and her knights slowly rise to their feet.

THUNDER HAND CONTINUES: We thank our king and his son as well for this opportunity to defend their honor and sovereignty. And we thank you for acknowledging our service to them and assisting you in this war. Our Lord Christ encourages you and all humanity to keep the same love for God in their hearts and to treat their fellow humans honorably. Very soon, The Christ will return and we will be with him to execute his righteous judgment upon the entire earth. We are proud to have fought with you today. All of you have greatly impressed all of us.

Then my brother Faith Speak, who is known in our realm above the stars as not only a fiercely loyal brother to our kings, but also the angel who sometimes talks too much, then excitedly says:

FAITH SPEAK: My Supreme brother speaks the truth. You have earned much respect from those of us who have witnessed your battles through the years and how valiantly you all fought today. I too, am proud to have gone to war with you today, and wish to show my sincere and heartfelt appreciation for my new favorite "heroes.".

Having said this, Faith Speak smiles warmly at Queen Splendina and her knights and starts to clap his hands very loudly. Then Michael and the four Supreme Seraphim smiles at them and they too started to applaud. Seeing their leaders are now applauding the knights and their queen, all of the angels surrounding them join in the praise. The deafening sound of millions of my brother angels clapping, cheering, and giving congratulations to the six earthly heroes fills my heart with joy and pride for them. In admiration I am of them because they all fought valiantly and bravely against the overwhelming odds of the evil Dark Soul and his hideous hordes, both in word and in deed.

Once again unknown to you humans, we angels have also commended humanity through its history. The very instant our Lord Christ died faithful and humble, all of heaven cheered and praised his firm, resolute commitment to his father and for being the savior of humanity. Also, when your human World War II ended, we approved very much. A war we hope will never happen again, in any form.

Many of us later agreed that neither the planet nor all the life on it would survive another war as terrible as that one. You humans have come much farther along in your creation of destruction and your weapons of war have become much more lethal to life on Earth as a whole.

The knights and their queen are now all smiles and wave back at the millions upon millions of my brothers. In awe and deep appreciation, they thank them over and over again. I am touched in spirit once again, because of their sincere humility towards us.

Slowly, Michael and the four Supreme Seraphim's turn around and start to gracefully fly upwards. A pathway is cleared for them through the great crowd of angels. As they fly upwards, my brothers follow. The applause becomes less and less as more and more angels leave, until all of them have disappeared back into heaven.

Once back in our dwelling place, all those who fought immediately gather in the grand Hall of the Heavenly Hosts. This is where we angels hold our meetings and where instructions are given out, plans are made and more. In your bibles, this enormous hall is mentioned several times. (1 Kings 22:19-22, Job 1:6,7 and Job 2:1,2) The size of this grand room is equal to seventy of the magnificent celestial galaxies your planet Earth presently resides in.

Always after a great battle, the angels who fought it are required to come together here to give an accounting of how they fought, to the archangel Michael and to discuss it among themselves too. But this meeting was special because Michael was also joined by the four Supreme Seraphim who also battled Dark Soul. Many times in the history of human warfare we have met here. Again, during your World Wars I and II, we were assembled for special and detailed instructions very, very often. Your human wars have caused this to happen, entirely too much in heaven.

Back on Earth, Queen Splendina and her knights are having a meeting of their own. She looks fondly at them and softly speaks:

QUEEN SPLENDINA: My devoted and dependable knights, I once again praise all of you for your service to our kings and to my heart. You were willing to give your lives for me and for all women through time. Bravely you all sparred against the unholy forces of Hell, led by the profane Dark Soul. To uphold our king's greatness and my honor your "glorious quest" (18) accomplished. You have truly lived up to your title, The Knights of Brave Love. I am sure that all of heaven has the same praise for you as well, and am greatly impressed with your true, raw courage.

PRINCE PASSION: My queen, it was truly a blessing from our kings to contend for their glory, and to fight for and with you. All praise to God and his son Christ for enabling us to be equal in power to that demented dog Dark Soul and his army from Hell. So blessed am I in your life "to be." (11)

SIR ROMANCE A LOT: I am in total agreement with my brother Prince Passion. It has always been a blessing to fight for our kings and through time, the hands of this man have had the chance to strive for your honor and also give you romance. (12)

RICHARD THE DEEP HEARTED: Add myself as well to all my brothers have said. My queen, through time and still today, my esteem for our kings and my love for you stands taller than the mountains and wider than the sky. Deeper than the ocean and more vast than the stars. (13)

BRAVE DUKE: I proclaim my allegiance to the one seated on the throne of heaven and to our Lord at his right hand. (Psalms 110:1, Hebrews 1:3) May their glory endure forever upon forever. I am just a man (14) who has loved you and fought to love you more. And today, to be by your side as we battled Dark Soul's hate and contempt for heaven and for love, was a privilege. All for God and for love.

BOLD KNIGHT: My adoring queen, each of my brother's has spoken what is in their hearts. I myself shall now reveal what lies inside mine.

I am also in absolute agreement with them. But I have more to tell you, my love. By the grace and greatness of our king and his beloved son, I was able to stand with you today against Dark Soul and his demonic hordes. And vanquish them we did, with the awe-inspiring help from heaven.

I have always been a protector of your precious heart. Together with my older brother Brave Duke, we swore an oath to guard you against the negativity that comes from living and loving every day through time. Mostly we have been successful in this endeavor. But sometimes we have failed. Win or lose, we fought hard as true men should to ensure your happiness. Like my brother Brave Duke has stated, I am just a man.

PART 4. A MAN SPEAKS

ACTION: Bold Knight changes into an ordinary man. I will let you the readers' imaginations decide what a man should be and look like.

A MAN: A man that now combines his title of Bold Knight and Brave Duke together inside himself.

And what they stand for: bravery, courage, and boldness to love an extraordinary woman as you.

ACTION: AFTER SAYING THIS, BOLD KNIGHT ABSORBS BRAVE DUKE INTO HIMSELF.

Brave at heart and courageous in soul your love has made me
A shining example for all to see

To defend your heart's honor as best as I can
Is the glorious quest of this modest man

Throughout time and human history
Your love has made me all I could be

That means watching over the love in your heart so pure
I never have to doubt its love is so sure

Against Hell itself today we have fought
And may this spectacular battle leave behind a lesson taught

That lesson is, love sometimes has to be fought over to be won
A man sometimes has to battle Hell and himself, from day one

To love a woman truly and deep

He may have to go to war, for her love to keep

Bold Knight and Brave Duke is with whom I have started
I now bring inside me Richard the Deep Hearted

ACTION: RICHARD THE DEEP HEARTED NOW GOES BACK INTO A MAN.

For he too has been a loyal, emotional friend
Whose love for you is boundless and has no end

To the stars and beyond is where his love goes
Even in the deepest sea, his love still flows

Yes, Richard has always been a part of me as well
All through time, his love for you has never failed

Bottomless, fathomless are words so profound
His love for you just cannot be bound

Deep in his heart too, your love has burned
In the hands of this man too, your love was hard earned (15)

Richard, Brave Duke, and Bold Knight, before they were three
Now inside this man they are one, loving you so free

Another heartfelt thanks to our heavenly sire
May his blessings add one more, whose love is required

ACTION: SIR ROMANCE A LOT IS MERGED INTO A MAN

He who is also needed, is Sir Romance A Lot
And his love like the others, burns for you so hot
Once again, he loves you "with ALL he's got"

He yearns to romance you with the sweetest of words
But he always remembers that love is also a verb

A verb means action, and its love he wants to show
To pour his heart into yours and let all its love flow

Dinner with soft music and candles on many a special night
Makes the love between us feel so right

To buy your favorite perfume, or a simple walk in the park
Helps us to stay in love and keep its spark

These are just a few things, but there is so much more
This humble man has to give you from his love store

The three now adds Sir Romance A Lot too
Inside this man, four are now as one who wants to love you

However, there is one more who wishes to join this" love cast"
Prince Passion is his title, and he is the last

ACTION: PRINCE PASSION IS NOW MERGED INTO A MAN. NOW A MAN STANDS BY HIMSELF WITH QUEEN SPLENDINA

The Prince of Passion and I am my queen's forever lover
Her sexy secrets I long to discover

For eternity, my love will always come first
Before we quench each other's "body thirst"

It's you and only you I crave and desire
Making love with you sets my soul on fire
A lovely feeling that will never expire

When we take each other to ecstasy's peak so high
My heart remembers** why you're the apple of my eye

I give praise and thanks to our wonderful King Eternal
For creating love as being much more than physical

Now all the Knights of Brave Love exist within the mind of A Man
To love a woman wholehearted as best as he can

All have become one in word, thought and deed
To be a true man, the one she needs

My queen, my lady, my friend, my lover
This man only wants you and no other

So blessed I am to love you because of God above
The magnificent and splendid creator of love

QUEEN SPLENDINA TAKES A MAN BY THE HAND LOOKS DEEPLY INTO HIS EYES AND SAYS:

I too give thanks to our King Eternal and his son
For creating this amazing feeling called love

It makes my heart soar above the clouds
Glide through the stars to the door of heaven itself
And knock on the door of its majestic throne room

My man,
All of the knights are back within you now
But you have constantly been my Knights of Brave Love

You have defended my honor and my heart (Bold Knight and his

"older brother" Brave Duke)
Inside of space and time you have loved me deeply (Richard the Deep Hearted)
Romanced me with words and action (Sir Romance A Lot)
Then made such sweet and tender love with me (Prince Passion)

I have also loved you, as you have loved me
The unfolding of time and love is within my soul too (17)
And just as we loved together, we also went to war together
For true love is NEVER easy, my dear
We have to fight against our own problems
Then to battle against a world that treats love so casual
As they misuse and abuse it in so many ways
Finally, to war against this world's unseen rulers and those visibly under their control

Despite all these obstacles, there are miracles
The miracle of being in love with you, my man

A MAN: My queen, I have loved you since Eden
When the Sovereign Lord Yahweh God first married us

ACTION: A MAN NOW GOES DOWN TO ONE KNEE, LOOKS QUEEN SPLENDINA DEEP IN HER EYES AND SAYS:

Lovely lady, today I ask again for your heart and your hand in holy marriage
As I have throughout time, and still do today
Still another blessing from our king and his loyal son

There is no clergy present to make this official
Before God and all of heaven as my witness, I proclaim my everlasting love for you

The Lord is our priest, our pastor
And Christ is our judge

BOLD EYE: I see what is happening between A Man and Queen Splendina. My heart is moved so very much, for I can feel the sincere and deep love they have for each other. And like he has stated, he has loved her since Eden and loves her even more today. I feel the spirit of The Lord in my ear. He says: "GO! and reveal yourself to them. You are to perform a special ceremony of marriage in my name and in the name of my son Christ Jesus."

Having heard those instructions, I, Bold Eye, the Archangel of the Cherubim, now leave the splendor of heaven and inside half a blink of an eye, instantly fly down to where A Man and Queen Splendina are standing. I reveal myself to them and the look in their eyes is again full of surprise and wonder.

I raise my hand over the head of Queen Splendina and she is instantly transformed from her battle armor, into The Century Princess again. But now she is clothed in a wedding dress that most of you humans wear in your ceremonies of marriage and love. (You the reader can use your imagination as to what type of dress she is now wearing)

I am now floating in front of the loving couple as they stand beside each other holding hands, with eyes full of love and adoration. Then I speak:

BOLD EYE: Your bravery and zeal has not gone unnoticed by God and The Christ. Neither has the love you feel for each other. The exceptional love you have felt for each other through time and today are the reason I presently stand before you. In the name of and with the blessings from the Almighty, I marry you once again. You may kiss to seal you union.

ACTION: THE CENTURY PRINCESS AND A MAN TURN TO EACH OTHER AND GIVE EACH OTHER A GENTLE KISS. THEN THEY TURN BACK TO BOLD EYE WHO SAYS:

Now bow your heads, place your left hands over your hearts, and raise your right hands in the air with your palms facing upwards to heaven.

ACTION: THE NEWLY, ONCE AGAIN MARRIED COUPLE FOLLOW BOLD EYE'S INSTRUCTIONS.

BOLD EYE: This gesture is the "SOS." The Sign Of Sovereignty. When it is done, it means that you recognize the greatness, glory, and grace of God in your hearts on this special day. May you humans remember this in your future marriage ceremonies.

My earthly brother and sister, may the undeserved kindness of the Savior Christ fill your minds and life together. I bid you farewell, for now.

ACTION: HAVING SPOKEN THOSE WORDS, BOLD EYE DISAPPEARS.

For a few moments, the newly, once-again married couple stands together as man and wife, taking in what has just happened. But from out of nowhere, the mocking voice of Dark Soul brings them back to their senses and reality.

DARK SOUL: Well, isn't that just lovely. Two horned frogs in love. Don't think that just because you had those hopping-in-my-affairs rabbits in heaven help you this time, that I will stay out of your life together. I am very persistent and I WILL return in some way to interfere and disrupt. Until my day of judgment, IT'S ON LIKE FOUR DONKEY KONG'S!

Also, if any of you humans think that it will be easy for you to permanently reside in heaven with your so-called Lord . . . think again. You all will have to go through my master and me and my wicked brothers first. And believe me; we will put you through hell and then more hell to break your faith.

THE CENTURY PRINCESS: Dark Soul, we know you are a rat and a cowardly snake. The word of God tells us that if we oppose you, that you will flee. (James 4:7, 1 Peter 5:8) But it also warns us to stay awake and be on guard against your attacks.

A MAN: My wife is right, you half-wit-maggot. We will continue to resist you and all your evil followers, up to the very moment of your destruction. (Revelation 20:7-10) Until then, we will rely upon our savior to help us defeat you and your dirty tricks.

Mankind has been fighting you since the rebellion in Eden, when your wicked master told the first lie we know of. We stand together with Christ in the middle, determined to battle you to our death, if need be.

THE CENTURY PRINCESS: Now go away, you big bat brained buzzard. This is our time alone together and no matter what you say, you will not steal our joy. You tried to once already, and look what came of it. If you keep talking, I will pray to God again for my armor and my weapons. **YOU KNOW YOU DON'T WANT ANY MORE OF THIS!!!**

BOLD EYE: In the heavenly realms, there is much laughter and joking because of what Queen Splendina just said to Dark Soul. Though they cannot see him now, we can, and the look of despair and humiliation on his face makes us laugh even harder. Yes humans, we angels also have a sense of humor like you do.

After laughing hard at Dark Soul, I gaze down from heaven and see A Man and his once-again bride-queen slowly walk off with arms around each other's middle, content in heart, soul, and spirit.

Once again, loud applause breaks out in heaven as I see millions upon millions of my angelic brothers applauding and cheering as they look down upon the happy couple. For reasons unknown to me, the heavens open up once more to reveal to A Man and his wife, all the myriads of angels who are congratulating them.

The couple stops walking and stares up in marvel and fascination. They both once again repeat the SOS (Sign Of Sovereignty) to the Celestial Sovereign Lord, Elohim God. Left hands over their hearts, right hands raised in the air with palms facing upwards, heads bowed in respect to God. The applause goes on for a few minutes longer, before the heavens close once more. Then there is silence.

One hand found the other and held it tightly as The Century Princess and her Knight of Brave Love joyfully stroll off into the radiant sunlight.

BOLD EYE THE ARCHANGEL: You have just read an amazing story (or "Play Post" as the poet Ed has termed it) of everlasting love, time, faith, determination, and a soon-to-be judgment upon your entire planet. Some of this is myth, but parts of this are very true and you can use your own bibles for verification. With this author's last book, its ending was the scriptures located at 1 Corinthians13, verses 4-7. In closing, I would like to repeat them here.

"Love is patient and kind; it is not jealous or proud. Love is not ill mannered or selfish or mean; love does not keep a record of wrongs. Love never gives up; and its faith, hope, and patience never fails."

I wish you all the best in life and in love.

One last thing. I have a strange feeling that this is not the last you will hear from me . . .

ED THE AUTHOR SPEAKS: You are right, Bold Eye, because The Eternal King Elohim God and his Faithful and True son Christ, You and ALL your loyal heavenly warrior brothers, Queen Splendina and her Knights of Brave Love will return in "Knights of Brave Love: Dark Soul Strikes Back."

THE MAGNIFICENT KING ETERNAL FINISHES THIS PLAY POST:

My children . . .All my precious children
You have just read a story that is part fable and part truth
From the mind of the one I inspired it came from

Do not let your differences in opinions and in beliefs cloud your minds to its truths
Know that love has conquered hate in the past (through Christ)
It is overcoming hatred in the present
And VERY soon, Christ will totally destroy ALL hate forever

Bold Eye performing the marriage ceremony of The Century
Princess and Bold Knight

A Man and The Century Princess perform The Sign Of Sovereignty

REFERENCES

All through my play post, you have seen numbers after certain words and phrases. This section will now explain what they mean and where they are located. Unless otherwise noted, all references come from my first book "Love, Sex, and Romance: Beautiful Love Poems for the Heart."

1. From my poem "Eyes of Forever."
2. From my poem "Of Love and Dreams."
3. From my poem "The Man That You Deserve."
4. Again from my poem "Eyes of Forever."
5. From my poem "The Love of a Lifetime Has Given Me a Lifetime of Love
6. From my poem "Beautiful Music, Beautiful Love (The Afterglow)."
7. From my poem "The Queen of My Dreams."
8. From my poem "The Other."
9. From my poem "The Hands of a Man."
10. From my poem "Of Mom and Oprah."
11. From my poem "To Be."
12. Again from my poem "The Hands of a Man."
13. From my poem "831."
14. From my poem "Just A Man."
15. Once again from my poem "The Hands of a Man."
16. From my poem "The Body Remembers."
17. From my poem "The Unfolding of the Two."
18. Richard the Deep Hearted quotes from the song "The Impossible Dream." (©) From the 1964 musical, "The Man of La Mancha." Composed by Mitch Leigh. Lyrics by Joe Darion. Performed by Andy Williams

** The reference on page 126 is from my poem "The Body Remembers" in my LSR book.

Ed Hendricks

WINNERS, HEROES, AND LOVERS

ABOUT THIS POEM:

The inspiration for this poem comes from the inspiring song "Winner In You" by Patti LaBelle. After listening to it in the past, I thought how it would be a good song to write a poem about, like I have done other songs in my Love, Sex, and Romance book. (Note: This poem IS NOT in my LSR book.)

But as I finished the writing of my play post here, I thought of how "Winner In You" would be a good fit for this book. As you have just read, The Knights of Brave Love (and later A Man) had to go through the forces of Hell to become The Century Princess's winner, hero, and lover. So I decided to include it as a bonus. I had to make a few changes in the original poem to fit it into my play post, but I made sure to keep the original meaning.

I am the happiest winner in the world
Because I can call you "my girl"

I have won over your mind and heart
And feel like "hero" is now my part

The hero of your heart is what I have now become
So glad that we two are now one

A hero's welcome is what your love feels like to me
For I had to fight through Hell, and make it flee

Brave in spirit I had to be
To win your love totally

Wielding the sword of patience and the shield of time
Prayers eventually came true, for you are now mine

So much I am in love with you
It's good to know you feel the same too

Nights into days, and days into nights
Love turns into passion that feels so right

The fire of love turns to desire
As two souls take each other higher and higher

Soaring past the clouds and to the stars
Ecstasy's highest peak is now where we are

Then basking in the moments of a romantic afterglow
Enjoying a reward of being your hero

Delighted I am that you chose to discover
I am your winner, your hero, and your lover

BONUS SECTION: MENTIONED POEMS

In this special section, I shall list in their entirety, some of the poems that The Knights and The Century Princess/Queen Splendina quoted from. Note that these are *some* of the poems from my first book "Love, Sex, and Romance: Beautiful Love Poems for the Heart."

OF MOM AND OPRAH

ABOUT THIS POEM:

This poem is about my admiration for two women that have inspired my life and touched it deeply. They are my mother, Ms. Dorothy B., and Oprah Winfrey. The idea for this poem came to me as I was thinking about people who I feel have left a positive influence on my life. In today's world, a lot of people tend to look up to some bad role models as their heroes. So I looked at my heroes and came up with these two wonderful ladies.

Two women whose lives are so separate, yet I see as equals

Oh mother,
Through my eyes I have seen your life unfold
I have witnessed your joys and pains
Your highs and lows, your strengths and weaknesses
I have seen your tears and caused your tears
I have seen those whom you loved wrong you, almost unto your death
Not an easy life you have led
But I still love you
And deeply respect you

Ms. Winfrey,
The eyes of the world have seen your life story
For we know how you rose from humble beginnings
Your successes and failures
Those you have helped and those that hurt you
We have felt your joys, and shared your pains
Yet you have remained strong
An amazing woman worthy of much praise

KNIGHTS OF BRAVELOVE

And like my mother, worthy of the deepest of respect

Oh ladies,
Separate yet equal I see you
Separate yet equal you have lived
Separate in lives, equal in emotion, struggle, and bravery

Through my eyes I have lived with you both
Admired you both
Respected you both
One for the love of son to a devoted mother
One for the love of an outstanding and inspiring human being

You ladies have overcome great odds
The powers of persistence, determination, and prayer were your allies
In becoming the fantastic women I see you as

You both have captured my heart
Dazzled my imagination
Ignited my inspiration
And enriched my life
Because of the way you have lived yours

My love goes out to you ladies
And may God bless you both

(Queen Splendina quotes from this poem)

THE QUEEN OF MY DREAMS

ABOUT THIS POEM:

My poem titled "The Mystery of Destiny" in my "Love, Sex, and Romance" book has a verse in it that reads:

"Ages upon ages ago I knew I loved you
For you are the princess of my centuries
You are the queen of my dreams"

So I took that last line and made it into its own love poem.

In the kingdom of my dreams
Where my life plays on my mind's screen
You are my queen

Thinking of you throughout the day
And as the light fades away
Now my imagination has full play

In this realm of the night
My heart takes to flight
How this feels, ever so right

Like the tales of knights of old
Brave at heart with courage so bold
My love for you is a story that must be told

But loving you is not a fairy tale
It is a feeling that I know so well
And deep in my heart is where it dwells

KNIGHTS OF BRAVELOVE

My nights are filled with thoughts of you
As well as the day we just loved through
And I know you feel this too

You are my queen, I am your knight
Like a hero, for your love I will fight
Even when my mind turns off its light

And at the end of your nightly reign
When I return to daylight's plane
The love for my queen will forever remain

(Richard the Deep Hearted quotes from this poem. **Notice the verses in bold print.**)

Ed Hendricks

BEAUTIFUL MUSIC, BEAUTIFUL LOVE (THE AFTERGLOW)

ABOUT THIS POEM:

After making love one afternoon and catching my breath, the title to this poem came to me. (Remember I said that inspiration can come at any time, any place!) So I wanted to write about my feelings on that lovely afternoon.

In the light of a slow, sunny afternoon

Soft music plays, we are off work today
Romance calls, clothes fall
Lips meet, hearts skip beats
Bodies touch, pulses rush
Making love starts and we both do our parts
Passion unfolds, ecstasy explodes
Climaxes are peaked and it's rest we now seek

Holding you close after the love we made
Enjoying the feeling of the passion we obeyed

Basking in the glow of something so beautiful
This for us was much more than physical

Mental, emotional, spiritual it was all of these combined
The ultimate expression of our love this moment in time

Energy is drained as we lay gasping for air
I now stroke your lovely hair

Beautiful music plays in the background

Helps to calm the body rush down

Snuggled around each other, feeling our hearts beat
The afterglow makes this love complete

And as that warmth covers us like a slow moving fire
Puts the finishing touch to our desires

The music, the love, and an afterglow so fine
We eagerly look forward to the next time

(Prince Passion quotes from this poem.)

Again, I apologize for the sensuality expressed.

THE STRENGTH OF A WOMAN

ABOUT THIS POEM:

The inspiration for this poem came from the song "A Woman's Worth" by Alicia Keys. Women all over the world have made much progress in many areas. In some things, they shine brighter than men. I see this as a sign of inner strength and wisdom and I just want to let ALL the women of the world know my thinking by writing this poem of great respect.

To Man,

I am WOMAN

WOMAN means **WO**rthy of **MAN**

I am MORE THAN worthy of your respect
Your praise, your admiration,
And your love

Mostly,I may not be stronger than you physically
But emotionally and mentally, I am more than your match
My strength is more inside than outside
For the world sees, feels, and knows my power

You cannot buy what I am worth, but you can earn it
With your respect, praise, admiration
   And love

WOMAN means being **With Our MAN**

I am with you because I WANT TO be with you

For you have EARNED my devotion
By your side I choose to be

NEVER behind you should I walk
Together we are as one
Completing and complementing each other

WOMAN means being **WO**nderfully **M**ade **A**nd **N**urturing

I nurture, I nourish, I protect
The wonder of creation lies within me
I was beautifully made for this purpose
And for many others, as you have already read about

You have trusted me to raise our children
Teach them, discipline them
Love them

For what I do for our children
I do for you as well

WOMAN means **W**isdom **O**f **M**any **A**ges **N**ow

I am wise in my own ways
Mostly different, sometimes the same as yours

Through the ages, my wisdom has been proven
Curie, Mother Teresa, Thatcher, and many others
Are the inspiring foremothers of today's women

Wisdom and nature always are one
Wisdom is also one of my natural abilities

I am WOMAN

I am **WO**rthy of **MA**g**N**ificence

And my strength

WOrks for the good of hu**MAN**ity

Special Note: I also would like to give a big shout out to the song "Respect" by Aretha Franklin. This song is the anthem for women all over the world to be treated with the respect and dignity they deserve. Even though it was recorded in the 60s, its message still holds true today. Thank you so very much Ms. Franklin. May you rest in peace.

And a SPECIAL shout out to the singer/actress Jennifer Hudson, who wonderfully portrayed Ms. Franklin in her biography movie. It would be very hard to find another actress on the planet, who could have played her better.

THE HANDS OF A MAN

ABOUT THIS POEM:

This is a poem I wrote for all the men out there that does manual work with their hands. I am talking about the auto mechanics, construction workers, carpenters, janitors, farmers, plumbers, etc., etc. Those of us who do hard with our hands have the scars to prove it. Yet our hands still have a "soft" side that we want our loved one to know about. This is my attempt to tell about that soft side.

Gazing at my hands
The years of toil tells on them
Working on this, working on that
They have paid the price

Hands that have done both good and bad
Hands that have done things they shouldn't have

Hands that have played and hands that have prayed
Hands that have fought hard and now are frayed

But now a blessing has come into these hands
A splendid treasure that is oh, so grand

For the love of a woman has been placed in them
In these hands a love like this has never been

A lovely thing of beauty and such grace
In this man's hands your love feels out of place

For how could these hands wrought with life's steel

Have opened your heart and to again love feel

How could such hands give you a loving touch
Together with its mind is in love with you so much

How could hands like this make love to you
When it's hard work that they are used to

But the hands of this man are asking for a chance
To light up your eyes and make your heart dance

The hands of this man are begging for a chance
To love you so much that your mind is entranced

The hands of this man pleads for the chance
To give you respect, honor, and yes even romance

   But most importantly...

Will this man have the chance in his life
To hold your hand in his, as man and wife?

(Sir Romance A Lot quotes from this poem)

JUST A MAN

ABOUT THIS POEM:

This is a poem I wrote about us men and our insecurities. At times we feel as if we are not good enough to be in love with a woman. Doubts come up because we place her on a pedestal so high that it makes us feel inferior to her. In this poem, I will try to explain those feelings.

I AM...

Just a man
Who wants to love you
Body and soul
Heart and mind
To love you with all I have
Spiritually, mentally, physically
To be in love with you
Day and night, always falling

For I am...

Just a man
A man whom is searching for the face of God
By doing what is right
By treating you right
That He may bless our love
So that we have a chance
To be together forever

For I am....

Just a man
A man who fights his fears
That he is not good enough

To love someone like you
Totally, completely, unconditionally
A man who yearns to touch your delicate skin
To hold your lovely body
To kiss your fair lips
To make love with you so passionately
For he feels so unworthy
Of such a marvelous beauty
Of such a natural splendor

For I am...

Just a man
Who longs to be closer than close to you
So near, but yet so far away
When I am with you
Into your mind is where I long to be
My hiding place is within your heart

Can this man be given the chance to do all these things with you?
For you? To you?
Can you forgive this man's shortcomings?
His fears?
His tears?

Will you hold him when he cries over you?
Will you scold him when you're mad at him?
But most importantly, will you still love him?

For I am...

Just a man

(Brave Duke quotes from this poem)

Ed Hendricks

THE LOVE OF A LIFETIME HAS GIVEN ME A LIFETIME OF LOVE

ABOUT THIS POEM:

I want to honor those who have been married for 30, 40, 50 or more years with this poem. One of the hardest things in life is to be married for a lifetime. I think very highly of those couples that have remained in love for years, and I wish them the best of love for the rest of their lives. I also wrote this poem from a man's point of view that has been in love with his wife all these years. This I feel is one of the greatest honors he can give her.

Decades ago we met, and fell in love
Time has flown by so fast
The kids have come and gone
"Grandma and Grandpa" the grandkids call us
Now it is just you and I

A lifetime of love you have given me
But it still seems like yesterday that I fell in love with you

Early in my life, I searched through the void for you
That vast, ever changing chasm of life
Persistence and prayer were on my side
In capturing your love

And as we lived and we loved through the years
I fell in love with you over and over and over again
My beautiful bride
My lovely wife
My loving mother
My exciting lover

Life was not easy for us
Staying in love has had its challenges
We have had our disagreements
The sun has shined on our love
The rain has fallen on our love
But through it all, we still are . . . in love

And now as we are in our golden years
And our bodies have become old
Though my vision is fading
My eyes still light up when they look into yours
The hands of this man are not as steady
But they hold firm when you take my hand

My Eternal Princess,
You have given me your heart
You have shared with me your heart and your soul
So blessed have I been for your lifetime of love
I now know for sure that you are the love of my lifetime
And may I take this wonderful feeling with me
When I go to meet God

EYES OF FOREVER

ABOUT THIS POEM:

Continuing with the theme of the eyes and love, we now come to the second poem in this series. In this poem I will introduce the concept of time and love. (Later in my book, you will read other poems about this concept)

Also I want to say that this poem has religious tones in it. I based this poem on the Bible verses at Revelation 21:1-4.

Right here, right now
I gaze into your eyes
The love that I see
Devotion that I feel

A thousand years from now
Love still shows in your eyes
Decades have passed
But our love has blossomed

Ten thousand years ahead
It's love that I still see inside your eyes
Time has changed so many things
But again our love has stayed the course

One hundred thousand years have passed
The love in your eyes is ever so bright
Millenniums have come and gone
But my love for you has still grown stronger

So much time has passed

Myriads of years, ages of centuries
And The Lord has blessed us
With his love and with our love
As The Ancient of Days he is timeless, boundless
He is time itself

But my love for you has grown deeper
I look forward to forever loving you
Being in love with you
Falling over and over and over again deeply
Every time I look into your eyes

We now stand at forever
As I gaze into your pretty eyes
Love still shines

Eons of time has gone by
Stars have died out
Galaxies have formed to become universes
Moving through time, space, and beyond
Worlds have been born anew

Earth has become the promised paradise
For the love of God is everywhere
And his love has been with us all this time
And now as eternity embraces us
We realize and know
That our love was meant to be

Forever

Always

Ed Hendricks

THE HEART TO WIN

ABOUT THIS POEM:

After watching Michael Phelps win gold medal number eight at the 2008 Summer Olympics, the thought came to mind to write a poem about what he and all the athletes went through to reach their peak. More inspiration for this poem came from Dara Torres, Usain Bolt, Bryan Clay, The USA Men's and Women's Basketball teams, the USA Women's Soccer team, and the Women's Marathon winner, Constantina Tomescu from Romania. These achievements were the ones that inspired me the most.

But this poem is not only for those who are in sports. This goes out to ALL who have strived to achieve a goal in life, ALL who have reached for their dreams, ALL who have had to overcome great odds to succeed.

"Conceive it, Believe it, Achieve it" is what they say
The challenge to be great, to do great things
Is the challenge life issues to all

"Where there's a will, there's a way"
I have the will to win
And the way before me has been set

But the way has been so hard
The road to glory so long
Filled with pain, disappointments, confusion
My frustrations have been many
Countless nights filled with tears
Followed by days of worry

"Should I stay the course?"
"Can I do this?"
"Why am I doing this?"
"Dare I attempt to achieve the impossible?"
So many questions, but few answers

My body bears the scars from the trials
Disciplined to its limits and beyond
So too was my mind
Pushed in ways I never thought possible
Stretched in ways I never dreamed of

How badly I wanted to give up
Many times I wanted to quit
But I kept my eye on the prize

"You can't do it"
"Give up now and settle for what you have"
"You will always be a _____ . Just be that"
Deep inside I knew I was better

Their unkind words fueled my determination
To be more, to do more
For they try nothing and always succeed
I choose to dare much
And stand a chance to win

I first saw failure as an enemy
And then later it became a friend
For a true friend teaches you lessons
Sometimes in the hardest way

But you have to leave some "friends" behind
And make new ones

Her name is Victory
His name is Success

For I have fought the fight of my life
Fear and doubt I always battled
Facing the danger of losing much
With courage beyond what is normal

The forces of Hell stood against me
Opposed to my majestic purpose
But faith and persistence sustained me
And God had mercy on me

Even in my darkest hour I knew there was a light
Now that light shines so bright on this great day

For my daring has paid off
All the years of hardship, of failures, are memories of the past
As success is now mine

I stand atop this magnificent pinnacle
Having realized the unlimited potential within
So wonderful of a feeling
So marvelous of an emotion
To have won at a goal in life

As excitement runs through my body
Knowing I faced overwhelming odds bravely
Knowing I overcame the insurmountable fortress of defeat
And won

And now, when I walk in the glory of the sun
I will hold my head high with a smile
And raise my hands to God

In eternal thanks

This ends "Knights of Brave Love: The Courageous Quest for Her Eternal Heart."

But The Century Princess/ Queen Splendina and her knights will return in "Knights of Brave Love: Dark Soul Strikes Back."

The totally evil and cruel demon Dark Soul returns with even more revenge. He has hatched a devious plot using The Anti-Christ, to turn even more of humanity against God and love. Included in his sinister plans are new adversaries, which our courageous heroes will have to do ferocious battle with. Heaven and Hell intensely collide, as the power of love and universal sovereignty is challenged once more. **Included in this amazing second book of the Brave Love series is something I don't think has ever been done, in human literary history. Stay tuned!**

To special order copies of this book, or to send me an email, please write to:

Tknob@Tknob.com OR QS@QueenSplendina.com

Queen Splendina and her Knights also have their web site at any of the following addresses:

TheKnightsOfBraveLove.com
TKNOB.com
QueenSplendina.com

Facebook page for Queen Splendina and her Knights of Brave Love, visit:

Facebook.com/BraveLoveKnights

You can also order copies of "Love, Sex, and Romance" on its web site at:

Lsrthebook.com.

Facebook page for Love, Sex, and Romance, visit:

Facebook.com/Lsrthebook and Facebook.com/LovePoems ByEd

Contact me about LSR at:

LSR@Lsrthebook.com

Lastly, copies of both books can be ordered on both sites.